faith
MATTERS
FOR YOUNG ADULTS

living the faith

Abingdon Press / Nashville

FAITH MATTERS FOR YOUNG ADULTS:
LIVING THE FAITH

Copyright © 2006 by Abingdon Press

All rights reserved.

This book is printed on acid-free, elemental-chlorine-free paper.

ISBN 0-687-49380-3

MANUFACTURED IN THE UNITED STATES OF AMERICA
06 07 08 09 10 11 12 13 14 15—10 9 8 7 6 5 4 3 2 1

Contents

Welcome to Faith Matters for Young Adults

Faith does matter! All adults—whether young, middle-aged, or older—yearn to believe in something. The psalmist wrote:

> "As a deer longs for flowing streams,
> so my soul longs for you, O God." (Psalm 42:1)

This resource begins with the basic assumption that human beings seek to ground their lives in something or someone beyond themselves. As Christians, we further believe that who or what is at the center of a person's life matters greatly.

Faith mattered to biblical people. Throughout the Bible, persons faced decisions concerning in what or in whom they should stake their lives and their souls. **Joshua** called the Israelites to choose whom they would serve—the gods of the Egyptians and the Amorites or the God who had led them out of slavery. **Elijah** forced the people of Israel to decide whether they would permit Baal or the Lord to shape their lives and destinies. **The prophets** called the people to change their lives, to move away from immorality, to choose instead lives of justice and righteousness that were worthy of the worship of the one true God. **Jesus** warned people that they could not serve two masters. He counseled that faith in God was better than shaping one's life around money or personal prestige. Faith continues to matter. Faith dictates the shape one's living takes.

If we think of the word *matters* as a verb rather than as a noun, we can say that faith takes substantial shape as we make choices and act day by day. Faith involves both belief and practice, in other words. Because we believe that God is just and merciful, we choose to be just and merciful. We practice serving others because we believe God in Christ calls us to serve others. Faith matters—takes shape—as we act upon what we believe.

You might also think about *faith matters* as referring to the actual topics of the sessions. What are the "matters" of faith? In three study books we offer sessions that will help view the Christian faith through three different lenses. Sessions in **Discovering the Faith** will help you learn more about matters related to the basic beliefs of Christian faith.

Sessions in **Practicing the Faith** will help you engage matters of faith through worship and participation in the ministries of a church, through the practice of Christian disciplines, and through the search for answers to challenging questions about God. Sessions in LIVING THE FAITH will help you explore what it means to live as a Christian and connect matters of faith to matters of everyday life.

Using the Books in Faith Matters for Young Adults

The titles of each of the sessions in *Faith Matters for Young Adults* are stated as questions. Adults of all ages have questions about faith and belief. Few expect to be satisfied with simple answers; however, it is important to engage matters of faith and belief by being willing to engage the questions. Such engagement, with God's presence and guidance, inevitably leads to faith development. Faith Matters for Young Adults seeks to help you engage the questions, discern what is at stake for your faith, and move you toward an understanding that will guide you as you grow in love of God and neighbor.

At the beginning of each book you will find:

– suggestions for starting a Faith Matters for Young Adults group.
– suggestions for different ways to use the book
– suggestions for leading a group

In each of the sessions you will find:

– a focus statement that illuminates the content of the session
– gathering and closing worship experiences related to the focus of each session.
– space to write reflections or insights evoked by topics in the main content.
– concise, easy-to-use leader/learner helps near the main text to which they refer.
– main content rich with illustrations from contemporary life and reliable information about the Scriptures in each session.

The three small-group study books in Faith Matters for Young Adults are designed for versatility of use in a variety of settings.

Small groups on Sunday morning (45 to 60 minutes). Sunday morning groups generally last 45 to 60 minutes. If your group would like to go into greater depth, you can divide the sessions and do the study for longer than seven weeks.
Weekday or weeknight groups (60 to 90 minutes). We recommend

90-minute sessions for a weekday or weeknight study. Participants should prepare ahead by reading the content of the session and choosing one activity for deeper reflection and study.

A weekend retreat. For a weekend retreat, distribute the books at least two weeks in advance. Locate and provide additional media resources and reference materials, such as hymnbooks, Bibles, Bible dictionaries and commentaries, and other books. If possible, have a computer with Internet capabilities on site. Ask participants to read their study books before the retreat. Begin on Friday with an evening meal or refreshments followed by gathering time and worship. Create a schedule that will allow you to cover the 13 sessions during the weekend.

Individual devotion and reflection. While the books are designed for small-group study, they can also be beneficial for individual devotion and reflection. Read the Scriptures, then read the main content of the sessions. Adapt the questions in the Leader/Learner boxes to help you reflect upon the issues related to the biblical theme.

Organizing a Faith Matters for Young Adults Group

Faith Matters for Young Adults is an excellent small-group study for young adults who seek to know more about the faith, about church, and about living one's faith in daily life. Some of these young adults may not be a part of a faith community, and yet they are seekers on a profound spiritual journey. They may be new Christians or new members who want to know more about Christian faith or who want to make new friends in a faith community. Or they may be people who have been in church a long time but who feel a need for spiritual renewal. This study invites all these young adults to engage more deeply with issues of faith and with the Bible in order to find meaning and hope.

Starting a Faith Matters for Young Adults study group is an effective way to involve young adults in the life of your local church. Follow the steps below to help you get started.

– Read through the Faith Matters for Young Adults study book. Think about the questions and the focus for each of the sessions. Prepare to respond to questions that someone may ask about the study.

– Decide on a location and time for your Faith Matters for Young Adults group.

– Develop a list of potential participants. An ideal size for a small group is 7 to 12 people. Your list should have about twice your target number (14 to 24 people). Ask your local church to purchase a copy of the study book for each of the persons on your list.

– Identify someone who is willing to go with you to visit the persons on your list. Make it your goal to become acquainted with each person you visit. Tell those you visit about Faith Matters for Young Adults. Give them a copy of the study book. Even if they choose not to attend the small group at this time, they will have an opportunity to study the book on their own. Tell each person the initial meeting time and location and how many weeks the group will meet. Invite them to become a part of the group. Thank them for their time.

– Publicize the new Faith Matters for Young Adults study through as many channels as are available. Announce it during worship. Print notices in the church newsletter and bulletin and on the church Web site, if you have one. Use free public event notices in community newspapers. Create flyers for mailing and posting in public places.

– A few days before the session begins, give a friendly phone call or send a note to thank all the persons you visited for their consideration and interest. Remind them of the time and location of the first meeting.

For more detailed instructions about starting and maintaining a small group, read *How to Start and Sustain a Faith-Based Small Group*, by John D. Schroeder (Abingdon, 2003).

Leading a Faith Matters for Young Adults Group

A group may have one leader for all the sessions, or leadership may be rotated among the participants. Leaders do not need to be experts in Bible study because the role of the leader is to facilitate discussion rather than to teach a particular content. Both leader and learner use the same book and commit to read and prepare for the session each week. So what does the leader do?

A Leader Prepares for the Session:

Pray. Ask for God's guidance as you prepare to lead the session.

Read the session and its Scriptures ahead of time. List questions or insights that occur during the reading. Make a list of any needed supplies.

Think about group participants. Who are they? What life issues or questions might they have about faith?

Prepare ahead. Gather any needed supplies, such as large sheets of paper, markers, paper and pencils, Bibles, hymnbooks, audiovisual equipment, masking tape, a Bible dictionary, Bible commentaries, a Bible atlas. Session 1 includes creating nametags and serving a simple meal. Gather supplies for making the nametags. Decide what kind of meal you would like to serve. Something like pizza or chili is easy to prepare and serve. If you are meeting in a classroom setting, arrange the chairs in a circle or around a table. Make sure everyone will have a place to sit.

Create a worship center. Find a small table. Cover it with an attractive cloth. Place a candle in a candleholder in the center. Place matches nearby to light the candle. Place a Bible or other items that relate to the session focus in the worship center.

Pray. Before the participants arrive, pray for each one. Ask for God's blessing on your session. Offer thanks to God for the opportunity to lead the session.

A Leader Creates a Welcoming Atmosphere

Hospitality is a spiritual discipline. A leader helps to create an environment that makes others feel welcome and that helps every participant experience the freedom to ask questions and to state opinions. Such an atmosphere is based upon mutual respect.

Greet participants as they arrive. Say their names. If the class is meeting for the first time, use nametags.

Listen. As group discussion unfolds, affirm the comments and ideas of participants. Avoid the temptation to dominate conversation or "correct" the ideas of other participants.

Affirm. Thank people for telling about what they think or feel. Acknowledge their contributions to discussion in positive ways, even if you disagree with their ideas.

A Leader Facilitates Discussion

Ask questions. Use the questions suggested in the leader/learner helps or other questions that occurred to you as you prepared for the session. Encourage others to ask questions.

Invite silent participants to contribute ideas. If someone in the group is quiet, you might say something like: "I'm interested in what you are thinking." If they seem hesitant or shy, do not pressure them to speak. Do communicate your interest. If one participant dominates conversation, remind the group that everyone's ideas are important. Again, invite those who are quiet to express their ideas.

Be willing to say, "I don't know." A leader is also a learner. You are not "teaching" a defined content to a group of "students." Instead, you are helping others and yourself to engage faith matters that emerge from discovering, practicing, and living Christian faith.

Session 1

What Does Living the Faith Mean?

Pamela Dilmore

FOCUS This session introduces the 13-week study, LIVING THE FAITH, a book in the series, Faith Matters for Young Adults. It will help young adults identify ways to live everyday life according to their Christian faith.

— GATHERING —

Create a nametag. On a small sheet of construction paper, write your name and one action or choice that is currently affected by your Christian faith or that might be affected by Christian faith. Use either masking tape or a straight pin to attach your nametag to your clothing. Find another person. Tell each other what you wrote on the nametag.

Share a meal, such as pizza or chili, with the group. As you eat, tell the large group about what you and your partner wrote on your nametags.

Pray together the Lord's Prayer.

Living Our Faith

What does it mean to "live" our faith? The reality of Christian faith is that it involves belief *and* action. Acting out of our belief involves all of our lives. *Discovering the Faith* offers opportunities to explore the content of the Christian faith. *Practicing the Faith* explores opportunities to learn about and to engage in traditional Christian practices that will nurture our faith in all of life, in the good times and in the difficult times. In it, we learn how to practice the spiritual disciplines associated with worship, Bible reading, prayer, service, and seeking meaning in the deep questions about ways God acts in our lives. This book, LIVING THE FAITH, explores what it means to live out the faith in down-to-earth ways in everyday life. This arena of action involves the choices we make everyday, choices that affect for better or for worse our relationships with God, with neighbor, with ourselves, and with all creation.

How do we know what choices to make? How do we determine what is right and what is wrong? Stop now and write about ways you respond to these questions:

As Christians, we seek God's guidance for our daily lives in the teachings and witness of Jesus Christ. God's care, God's saving activity, and God's nature are revealed in the life, ministry, teaching, death, and resurrection of Jesus Christ. In the Bible we discover the laws given by God to guide those who wish to live as God's people. God offers us a "way of being and acting" in our world according to God's ways of mercy, hope, justice, and love. Grounded in the biblical principles, we use God's gifts of reason, consider our experience, and look to Christian tradition to inform our decisions.

The Ten Commandments

The Ten Commandments define the covenant relationship between God and the chosen people and the way that God's covenant people are meant to relate to one another. They are also called the "Decalogue" or "Ten Words" and are recorded in Exodus 20:1-17 and Deuteronomy 5:6-21. In Exodus the Ten Commandments are written by God on Mount Sinai on two stone tablets. Moses takes the tablets down the mountain to the people. In Deuteronomy, Moses recites the Ten Commandments in the context of remembering how God made a covenant with them. Moses' recitation of this history precedes his last will and testament to the covenant people.

The Ten Commandments are all about the health and wholeness of the covenant community. They offer guidance for relationship with God, family, and neighbor. *Harper's Bible Dictionary* calls them "fenceposts" supporting the fence that protected the people from chaos. They are intended for the preservation of the community.

Form two teams. Team 1 read the Ten Commandments in Exodus 20:1-17. Team 2 read the Ten Commandments in Deuteronomy 5:6-21. What do the commandments say to you about relationship with God? with family? with neighbors? Share the highlights of your conversation with the entire group.

The commandments that define the relationship with God clarify that God is greater than humans and cannot be manipulated by humans. God requires exclusive worship. Idolatry is prohibited. God's name is not to be placed into human service and control. One day a week, called the sabbath, is to be consecrated as a holy day for rest and relationship with God. The commandment to honor one's father and mother insures integrity of the family unit, most fundamental in society. Injunctions against murder, adultery, theft, false witness, and covetousness insure the integrity of the community. All such actions threaten the wholeness of the covenant community.

Obedience to the Ten Commandments is meant to be an expression of gratitude and praise to the God who initiated and defined the covenant relationship rather than slavery or servitude to an arbitrary deity. In the Ten Commandments, God defines the character of the relationship and calls for free and grateful obedience. The large principle here is that the integrity of covenant community depends upon a healthy relationship with God and neighbor.

The Ten Commandments offer basic principles of healthy relationship in contemporary Christian communities as well as in communities at large. Think about their relevance and the guid-

Session 1: What Does Living the Faith Mean?

ance they offer to individuals and communities. Consider what they mean to you. How do the Ten Commandments offer guidance for you and your daily choices? Write some of your thoughts in the following space:

The Great Commandment

In an effort to test Jesus, an expert in the law of Moses, probably a scribe and a member of the group called the Pharisees and a person we would call a "lawyer" in our culture, asked Jesus a question. Matthew 22:36 and Mark 12:28 record a similar question: Which law is greatest or first of all? Luke 10:25 frames the question in a slightly different way: "What must I do to inherit eternal life?" All three Gospels give a scriptural response based on Deuteronomy 6:5, "You shall love the Lord your God with all your heart, and with all your soul, and with all your mind"; and Leviticus 19:18, "You shall not take vengeance or bear a grudge against any of your people, but you shall love your neighbor as yourself: I am the LORD."

> Form three teams. Team 1 read Matthew 22:34-40. Team 2 read Mark 12:28-34. Team 3 read Luke 10:25-28. What insights do these Scriptures offer about ways to live a Christian life? Read the Scriptures aloud in the entire group. How are they similar? How are they different? After reading and discussing the similarities and differences in the Scriptures, share with the entire group the highlights of your team's conversation about ways they help us live a Christian life.

In Matthew and Mark, Jesus answers the question. In Luke, Jesus calls upon the lawyer to answer the question, affirms his correct response, and offers the parable of the good Samaritan as an illustration. Christians have traditionally referred to the teaching in these three Gospels as the Great Commandment.

Faith Matters for Young Adults: Living the Faith

Take some time now and prayerfully read Luke 10:27. In the following space write or draw about any thoughts, images, or feelings that come to you about how you might use the Great Commandment as a guide for living the Christian faith from day to day.

Jesus' life, teachings, and daily actions illustrate the heart of the Great Commandment and provide a powerful witness for living as a Christian. Jesus demonstrated both love of God and neighbor when he healed people, when he taught them, and when he sought to be obedient to God in all his words and actions. Through his life, ministry, death, and resurrection, he reveals the God who is just, compassionate, and merciful to all. He demonstrates the God who forgives, transforms, and saves us. What stories about Jesus in the Gospels offers you the best role model for how you might live your daily life? Write about your thoughts or feelings below:

Insights of the Early Church

Acts 2:42-47 offers a glimpse of the communal life of the early followers of the "way" of Jesus. In this Scripture, it is clear that these early worshipers made connections between the life of worship and daily life. Read Acts 2:42-47. List ways that these early followers "lived" their life of faith.

The apostle Paul offers great insight into what it means to live as a Christian when he writes letters addressing specific issues in the churches. Many of his teachings are timeless interpretations of what it means to live the Christian faith and continue to offer guidance to contemporary Christians. Look at the following Scriptures. What insights do they offer to you about living the faith?

What connections do you see between Paul's writings on how to live as a Christian and the Great Commandment? the Ten Commandments? How might these writings affect the choices you make as you live your faith?

1 Corinthians 13

Galatians 5:16-23

Ephesians 4:25—5:2

Philippians 4:8

1 Thessalonians 5:8-22

God Is With Us

Through Christ, God's Holy Spirit empowers and sustains us as we make choices and act upon them. As we claim the rich, life-giving realities that God offers to us through Christ, we also claim the invitation to live our faith with courage and hope. We respond to God's call with our daily choices and actions. We make connections between what God has done and continues to do through Jesus Christ, connections that help us to live our faith day by day. Our faith, which is God's gift of grace, increases our desire to love and serve God and neighbor.

Looking Ahead

The sessions in LIVING THE FAITH deal with specific issues that are likely to be a part of everyday life. Sessions 2, 3, and 4 offer help for dealing with stress, crisis, and change. Sessions 5–7 focus on ways we can care for the body and what behaviors could be harmful to the body. Sessions 8–13 deal with various aspects of human relationships. Sessions 8–10 look at sexuality, intimacy, singleness, marriage and divorce. Sessions 11–12 offer help with forgiving others or seeking for-

> Sing a hymn about living one's faith such as "Lord, I Want to Be a Christian" or "I Want Jesus to Walk with Me."

giveness. Session 13 looks at ways God mends a broken heart. All these sessions are designed to help us realize more deeply that our actions have effects on ourselves and on those around us. They help us explore ways to live our faith in order to promote God's good for all people and all creation.

– CLOSING WORSHIP –

Pray together the following prayer or one of your own:
"God of all life, we want to live day by day as your people. As we study the sessions, help us to hear what you have to say to us about living as a Christian. Help us to look to Jesus, who showed us who you are and who you call us to be; in Christ we pray. Amen."

Session 2

How Can Christians Handle Stress?

Larry F. Beman

FOCUS This session helps young adults discover ways the Christian faith can help them respond to the stresses in their lives.

⁻ GATHERING ⁻

Use a variety of art supplies, such as large sheets of paper, colored markers or crayons, colored paper, scissors, and glue or tape. Create a symbol or other drawing to represent what stress means to you. When you have completed your symbol, tell the group about your symbol.

Read aloud Philippians 4:6-8.

Pray together the following prayer:
"God of hope and comfort, be with us as we explore stress in our lives. Help us as we discover ways to respond to stress. Give us faith in your presece and care. In Christ we pray. Amen."

The Ups and Downs of Stress

Stress! It is a leading cause of heart disease; it energizes people to reach to new heights. It debilitates; it creates. It is loathed; it is welcomed. The truth is that stress has up sides and down sides. Stress is a set of physical and mental responses caused by something external. These may include increased heart rate, rise in blood pressure, muscular tension, irritability, or depression. On the positive side, such responses are the body's way of preparing to act; however, sustained stress can lead to bad health.

Think about the definitions of stress and its ups and downs. Consider the stress points in your life. How has stress limited you? empowered you? Do you see stress as good or evil? What does your personal faith tell you about stress? Take a moment and write or draw your responses below.

What are some words you use to describe stress? List responses on large sheets of paper or a chalk-board. What do the responses say about stress? How many of the words are negative? How many are positive?

Stress is a human response to fear. Fear is one of our basic emotions and a driving force in our life. If an event in our life is not fearful, we will not feel pressured by it. Our fear comes from a variety of sources. We might fear failure. We might feel we do not measure up in a situation. We might fear not being loved. Only when we begin to identify our fears can we respond to the workings of stress. Any discussion of stress needs to include a conversation about the fears that live within us. What basic fears do you associate with the stress points in your life? Write about your insights below:

Find a partner. Talk together about fear and stress. What connections do you see between the two? Make a list of other fears. When you are finished, share your list of fears with the entire group.

Name Your Dragons

One way to look at fear is through the metaphor of dragons. In the history of Western culture, dragons have frequently represented the fearful places of life. Sailors used to mark the uncharted seas with the words, "Here be dragons." Since dragons were viewed as enemies, the heroes of the West often rode off to battle these monsters. In one such story Saint George rescues a princess (who is about to be sacrificed to a dragon as an appeasement) by slaying a fire-breathing dragon with a powerful magic sword.

In the Eastern world, however, dragons are viewed differently. Instead of enemies to be killed, dragons are friends to be honored. The dragon even appears as a national symbol and an important part of special ceremonies.

Perhaps we need to look at fear less as an enemy to be destroyed and more as a friend to be honored. Perhaps we could begin to reduce the power that stress has over us if we began to name our dragons, talk with them, celebrate their presence, and let them guide us. In this way fear would become not a tyrannical god to whom we pay homage but a friend with whom we share our life.

Find a partner. Talk about your dragons. How is the cause of your stress like a dragon? Why is "naming your dragon" a helpful tool? What can you do to turn your stressful situations into friendly dragons? To what extent would you be changing the situation? To what extent would you be changing your attitude toward the stressful situation? What insights did you gain from naming your dragons?

In the following space, draw outlines of two or more dragons. Write on each dragon the things that give you stress. If possible, identify the underlying fear that creates that stress. In other words, name your dragons. Decide whether each dragon is a friend to be embraced or an enemy to be feared. Decide how you will respond to your dragon. Write your thoughts near each of the dragons you named.

How Can the Bible Help With Stress?

Friendship with fear finds life in the Christian faith when we realize the enormous power of four fundamental principles:

Deuteronomy 6:4-6. God is God. As the Hebrew people have said for centuries, "The LORD is our God, the LORD alone" (Deuteronomy 6:4). Stress is not God. Neither are the underlying influences that create stress. There is one—and only one—God.

Genesis 1:26-31. God created us, blessed us, and called us and all creation "very good." Our emotions are part of God's gift of who we are. One of these emotions is fear.

John 3:16-17; 1 John 4:7-12. We are loved by God—unconditionally. The central message of the gospel is that God's grace is available as a gift. There is nothing anyone can do to earn this love; the only thing necessary is to accept it.

> Form four teams. Team 1 read Deuteronomy 6:4-6. Team 2 read Genesis 1:26-31. Team 3 read John 3:16-17 and 1 John 4:7-12. Team 4 read Exodus 19:3-6. What connections do you see in the main idea of the Scripture and stress? Each team tell the entire group about the highlights of their discussion.

Exodus 19:3-6. God promises salvation in the present tense. Both the Old and New Testaments are filled with affirmations of God's power to rescue all God's people and to restore them to wholeness. In this wholeness we are set free. We can test our wings again and again, knowing that God, who is described in Exodus as a parent eagle, will hover over us to catch us when we fall out of control.

Other Scriptures offer insights that can inform our thinking about stress. Read each of the following Scriptures. What is the key idea in this passage? What do you think this passage has to do with stress? Does this passage help you deal with stress or not? If so, how is it helpful? If not, why is it not helpful?

Psalm 42

Psalm 121

Matthew 6:25-34

Romans 15:13

1 Corinthians 15:58

Galatians 5:1

What Can I Do to Reduce Stress?

In addition to biblical insights and beliefs about God that under-
gird Christian faith, people can do a number of practical things to reduce negative kinds of stress. Simple health habits are a perfect beginning place. Do you eat a balanced diet? Are you getting enough sleep? Do you exercise daily? What changes can you

> Create a group list of ways to respond to or reduce stress. Which ways do you use regularly? Which ones would you like to try? How do these ideas relate to the Scripture passages you read earlier?

make to adapt these habits of good health? Learning effective ways to manage work, school, and daily life can reduce unneces-sary stress. Do you have a plan for your day? Can you prioritize your tasks? What has to be first? What can wait? Christian spiri-tual practices like prayer, meditation, and reading the Bible everyday can still the body and calm the soul. When can you take time to pray? to read the Bible? to simply be with God in a quiet way? List other things you might do to reduce stress.

The Christian faith offers much that can be helpful to anyone who must deal with stress, either positive stress or negative stress. A person who truly lives with trust in the God who saves us, supports us, helps us, and is with us through Jesus Christ is well equipped to manage stress in daily life.

– CLOSING WORSHIP –

Read aloud the following Scripture:
"Who will separate us from the love of Christ? Will hardship, or distress, or persecution, or famine, or nakedness, or peril, or sword? As it is written,
  'For your sake we are being killed all day long;
    we are accounted as sheep to be slaughtered.'
No, in all these things we are more than conquerors through him who loved us. For I am convinced that neither death, nor life, nor angels, nor rulers, nor things present, nor things to come, nor powers, nor height, nor depth, nor anything else in all creation, will be able to separate us from the love of God in Christ Jesus our Lord" (Romans 8:35-39).

Pray silently about ways you might use Paul's insights to address the stresses in your life.
Close the session by praying the Lord's Prayer.

Session 3

How Does the Chrisian Faith Help Me Cope With Crises?

Larry F. Beman

FOCUS This session explores the resources of the Christian faith in order to help young adults find ways to cope with the unexpected crises of life.

– GATHERING –

Ahead of time write the word "crisis" on a large sheet of paper or a chalkboard. Place this in an easily accessible location. On this poster, all group members write about or draw sketches of what the word *crisis* suggests. When everyone has written or drawn on the poster, review the responses in the entire group.

Read aloud the following Scripture: "And remember, I am with you always, to the end of the age" (Matthew 28:20b).

Pray together the following prayer:
"God of hope and salvation, help us find assurance in your presence as we cope with the crises of our lives. In Christ we pray. Amen."

Crisis! The word blasts into our consciousness to blot out all other thoughts. Routines are disrupted. Lives are forever changed. This session will explore some of the dynamics of crises, looking at such radical events through the eyes of the Christian faith. As you work through this session, consider the following ideas: How do you usually respond in a crisis? Are you one who holds up well until the event is over and then falls apart? Do you go to pieces? Are you stoical? emotional? decisive? confused? Write brief responses in the following space.

Chances are you have a relatively consistent response pattern. The way you respond to one crisis is probably the way you will respond in other situations. Your pattern of response has either conscious or subconscious advantages for you or else you would not use it. Your pattern likely has limitations as well; these limitations will hold you back from responding in the ways you feel should be the most appropriate for you. So it is important to be "in tune" with yourself—your attitudes, your beliefs, your usual response patterns. It is also important to realize that each of us responds to crises in different ways, based on personality and family history. While some *behaviors* may be appropriate or inappropriate, our *response patterns* are neither right nor wrong. They just are.

Form teams of two or three. Use the following questions as discussion starters: How do you usually respond to a crisis? What are the advantages of your response pattern for you? What are the limitations? If you could change one thing about your response pattern, what would it be? What would you keep the same?

Case Studies of Crisis Events

Crises in life take many forms. The following case studies illustrate the crises of death, job loss, and failing an exam. Read each of the case studies. Think about how each person responds. What feelings or thoughts do you have about each situation and how each person responds? How would you respond? What do you believe the Christian faith has to say in each situation?

Crisis 1: The call came just after lunch. There had been a terrible accident. She had died instantly. We were so sorry. In the days that followed, he was numb. He made the preparations for the funeral mechanically and without feeling. He felt he needed some level of understanding of what had happened, so he told people, "It was God's will. God wanted her in heaven more than I needed her here." In the months that followed, he became furious with God.

Crisis 2: She arrived at work one morning to discover a note on her desk asking her to report to the personnel office. "We are sorry," they said, "but business is slow. We are going to have to lay you off. You can go home as soon as you have cleaned out your desk." She did not know what to say, so she simply left. For a while, she looked at the want ads in the newspapers. She even thought of working with an employment agency. But her lethargy kept her from making any movement at all. Over and over, she said to herself, *If I wasn't good enough to do that job, I'm not good for much of anything.*

Crisis 3: He was going to be the first person in his family to graduate from college. His parents were so proud of him that they were planning a huge party. All he had to do was complete one more course. But that course was the most demanding of his college career. He worked hard to pass. This morning, in class, his final paper was returned to him, marked with an *F*. Now he was walking the sidewalk of his campus alone. What would he do? What would he tell his family? How could he go on? Why was he such a failure?

Crisis in the Bible

How did people of the Bible respond to crises? Read each of the Scriptures and write responses to the questions that follow.

The Book of Job asks, Why do good people suffer? Curiously, the question is never answered. Instead, God is affirmed as God. When Job realizes this simple fact, he returns to wholeness. Read Job 1:13-19; 6:1-9; 38:1-7. If you were in Job's position, do you think you would you respond in the same ways he did? What might you do differently? What does this Scripture reading tell you about living through crisis?

Psalm 42 comes from the time of the Exile. The people of Israel believed God was a "located" god whose home was in the Temple in Jerusalem. When they were taken into captivity, they believed they left their God behind. The greatest discovery of the Exile was that God went with them and lived with them in their anguish. The psalms from this period are therefore filled both with anguish and a deep current of belief. Read Psalm 42. What emotions do you hear in this psalm? How do they compare with the ways you feel during a time of crisis? What does the psalmist say that is most important to you?

In Romans 8:31-39, we read that Paul was no stranger to crisis. Having been shipwrecked, jailed, and beaten, he had known some of the worst experiences of life. Out of these experiences, he was able to say that nothing could ever separate us from God's love. Read again Romans 8:31-39. What do you think Paul is saying? Where do you agree with him? Where do you disagree or have questions? What do you hear that is most helpful to you as you face crises?

Form 3 teams. Team 1 read Job 1:13-19; 6:1-9; 38:1-7. Team 2 read Psalm 42. Team 3 read Romans 8:31-39. Each team discuss the questions listed in paragraphs related to each of the Scriptures. Write a group prayer based on your reading and discussion of the Scripture. Read your prayer to the entire group.

Holy Week as a Model for Living With Crisis

The climactic events of Holy Week as described in Matthew 26–28 are powerful symbols for life in a time of crisis. Read the sequence of crisis events in these chapters. Each moment is important and inescapable. Read about each of the events from the following story. Remember a time when you were in crisis. Using that memory, complete the statements in each part of the crisis sequence.

The Last Meal

First comes the "night of last things." If an ending or death is imminent and known, people say their goodbyes and perhaps have a last meal together. If the crisis comes suddenly, this "night of last things" is seen only in retrospect.

I said goodbye when

Some things I did were

I felt

The Day of Dying

The "night of last things" is followed by the "day of death." Here there is agony, anguish, pain, and sometimes death as the crisis unfolds. Emotions are raw. Shock is often a close neighbor.

The crisis event took place when

My reaction was

My emotional response was

The Day of Waiting

The "day of death" is followed by the "day often forgotten"—the time of waiting. Events of the crisis begin to be sorted out in this period of lying fallow. Healing seems delayed, and persons often wonder if they will ever be whole again. This period frequently has a heaviness about it, a feeling that a weight too heavy to carry is being moved grudgingly forward. Even though people do not like this time of waiting, this critical period needs to be approached with as much patience as it is possible to muster.

One thing I remember about this period was

I often

I really thought

The Day of Resurrection

The "day of resurrection" tiptoes into consciousness as a surprise. On that day, persons wake up to discover they are able to function again. The sun is shining. Life has a new meaning. The crisis may have left scars, but there is strength in the scar tissue. Words such as *peace, energy,* and *hope* creep into one's sentences. All of life is colored by the dawn.

I discovered I had reached this point when

I felt

One thing I did was

Reflections

As we think back to past crises in our lives, we often discover new insights about what happened and how we grew through the experience. Take a moment now to consider what you learned from your crisis.

Looking back, I think

One thing I learned was

I believe God

When future crises occur, I expect

"I Am With You Always"

The Holy Week crisis sequence in Matthew's Gospel concludes with a surprising message: There is no abandonment! Even though we may feel terribly alone, God is with us each step of the way. God is in the goodbyes, the dying, the waiting, and the Resurrection. The promise of the Scripture is fulfilled: "I am with you always" (Matthew 28:20).

⊢ CLOSING WORSHIP ──

Think of words and phrases describing God's help in our life during times of crisis. Responses might include words such as *faithful, present, comforting,* and so forth. After each suggested word, say together, "Even though I walk through the darkest valley, I fear no evil."

Close the session with the Lord's Prayer.

Session 4

How Can Christians Deal With Change?

Larry F. Beman

FOCUS This session will help young adults identify their feelings, attitudes, and responses to change. It will help them explore the help God offers for coping with change.

- GATHERING ──

Ahead of time place a large sheet of poster paper or a chalkboard in an easily accessible location. Write the word "change" for all to see. Group members write words or draw images of a change you have experienced in your lives in the last five years. Tell one another about what you wrote or drew. How did these changes affect you personally? Which ones did you initiate? Which do you feel were imposed on you? Which changes were the most significant for you? What is your usual response to change?

Pray together the following prayer:
"God of courage and hope, some of us are fearful of change; others of us are motivated and excited by change. Help us to look at change as opportunity. Give us trust and faith as we explore what it can mean to us; in Christ we pray. Amen."

Change--A Fact of Life

Do you remember when all telephones were wired into telephone lines? when all televisions were attached to antennas? when organ transplants were an experimental dream? when the only way to send a letter was through the mail? Change—for better or for worse—is a fact of life. Its pace appears to be accelerating yearly, and the foundations on which we once built our lives seem to be made of shifting sands. Some things we once took for granted are now obsolete. Along with this obsolescence has come a changing value system.

One of the most helpful things we can do for ourselves is to identify the ways we think and feel about change. When we can put words around our attitudes, we can begin to make choices about how we will deal with change. This session will give you an opportunity to explore your feelings and attitudes toward change. You will be using a tool called "values clarification" as you work through the session. You will stretch your imagination, make choices, and clarify your beliefs about change and uncertainty. Take a few moments to write quick responses to the following questions:

How do you respond when change happens? Do you welcome change? Do you fear it? Do you resist it?

What difference does it make to you to say, "I believe in God," when you are living in a time of uncertainty?

Explore Attitudes About Change

Work through the following exercises to help you identify your attitudes about change.

Session 4: How Can Christians Deal With Change?   37

Circle the one response to each statement that best represents your opinion.

A. Change is most like
    1. a river
    2. an ocean
    3. a waterfall
    4. a flood.
B. Change is like the game of
    1. dominoes
    2. Simon says
    3. hide and go seek
    4. volleyball
    5. chess
C. A road sign that best describes my feeling about change is
    1.a crossroads
    2. a stop sign
    3. a detour sign
    4. a yield sign
    5. a one way sign
D. In my response to change, I am most like
    1. a fisherman steering a motorboat
    2. a sailor tacking in the wind
    3. a person paddling a canoe
    4. a passenger on a ship
E. Faith, during change, is
    1. knowing the lights will come on when you turn on the switch
    2. exercising with a friend
    3. shopping in a favorite store
    4. calling a family member on the telephone
F. During times of uncertainty, I think of God mostly as
    1. an eagle
    2. a light
    3. a parent
    4. a rock
    5. a fortress

Faith Matters for Young Adults: Living the Faith

Check the one statement in each pair of sentences that is closest to your belief.

A. _____ I approach change with fear and trembling.
_____ I approach change with excitement and anticipation.

B. _____ I am more likely to initiate change than to resist change.
_____ I am more likely to resist change than to initiate change.

C. _____ During uncertain times, I sometimes wonder if God cares.
_____ During uncertain times, I know God is with me.

Place an X on the lines that follow at the spot between the two opposites that most accurately represents your opinion.

> Find a partner. Review your responses to the activities. What insights did you gain from exploring your attitudes about change?

A. Insisting on certainty in a time of change is
Careful planning _____Rigidity

B. Living peacefully with uncertainty during a time of change is
Flexibility _____ Lack of direction

C. During change, God is
Letting me make   Always showing me
my own decisions_____the way

Reflect on Statements About Change

Following you will find several statements concerning change. Think carefully about them. Choose two or three that appeal to you or that say something important to you about change.

"When it comes to change, you do the best you can, and you cry a lot."

"Sometimes change means giving up what I want and listening to what God wants."

"Miracles occur when you start to recognize them."

"I look at the worst-case scenario. I figure if I can handle that, I can handle anything."

"God walks beside me even in the midst of my uncertainty."

Why did you choose the statements you chose? What insights do they offer? How would your life be affected if you approached change in the way the statement suggests?

"My Christian community supports me during times of change."

"Change is part of God's continuing creativity."

What Does the Bible Say?

Christian faith has much to offer in order to help us respond in positive ways to change. Three Scripture passages are especially helpful as we consider the dynamics of change.

Read Genesis 1:1-3. What possibilities do you see for creative change to emerge from chaos? Looking back, have you created something new more often during times of uncertainty or during times of stability? What does this Scripture say to you about change?

The first is the Creation story of Genesis 1:1-3. As the story begins, the universe is formless. The image found in Genesis is one of blackness and storm. Deep waters are raging, and agonizing darkness is everywhere. In the Hebrew world the oceans were seen as places of terror. God moves over this chaos and uses the turmoil as a threshold for creativity. Out of chaos comes new life.

The second Scripture is Ecclesiastes 3:1-15. Here the writer of Ecclesiastes, the Teacher, who often sounds like a whining pessimist, views change as inevitable. Yet, in these verses he speaks volumes about the reality of change in his world—change that was taking place more than 2,500 years ago. It appears that he saw change as a reality that is neither good nor evil. His

Faith Matters for Young Adults: Living the Faith

questions were these: Since there is change, what do we do about it? And what place does God have in this world of change? For him each period of change has its season, its own special time. Change just happens. Yet, all things are suitable for their time. We cannot understand why they come or go, but we can be sure that all is in God's hands. All that we observe and do has meaning in the ultimate plan of God.

> Read Ecclesiastes 3:1–15. How do you respond to this Scripture? Where do you agree or disagree with the "Teacher"? Since there is change in your world, what do you think is the most appropriate way to respond to it? Where do you believe God is or is not involved in change? What insights about change does the Scripture offer to you?

The third Scripture is Hebrews 11. Faith, for this writer, is more than a passive thought process. Faith, in these verses, is more than mere belief. Faith is a verb. People in the Scripture act out of trust, take risks, and embrace change as possibility and opportunity. Although some of these faith heroes appeared to be out-of-their-mind fools at the time, history proves that their faith-filled risk-taking made all the difference as they stepped into the future. In the world of these people, faith meant energy and empowerment more than it meant peacefulness and stability. It was a way of life for these persons who moved ahead in the midst of a threatening world. Faith, then, is active, not passive. Faith is energy more than it is stability or tranquility. It is courage to act out of one's trust in God.

> Read Hebrews 11. Do you agree or disagree with the ideas in this paragraph about faith? What challenges you about this Scripture passage, or about this paragraph? What excites you? How does the Scripture offer insights about change?

God Is With Us

The message of the Christian faith is that God's people have a rock on which to stand even when all else seems uncertain. This rock is the constant presence and love of our Creator God. God walks with us through changing times, remains connected to us, and offers presence and empowerment as we reach into tomorrow. We see many examples of God's steadfast presence and love in the stories of God's people. We see the powerful, life-giving, saving power of God through Jesus—through his life, ministry, death, and resurrection. Whatever change we encounter in life, we can be assured that God does not abandon us. God loves us and offers us support.

– CLOSING WORSHIP –

Take a moment to pray silently about the changes in your life. Imagine that God is speaking to them personally. Write in a few words or sentences what you believe God is saying to you as you face the changes and uncertainties of life.

Close by reading the following affirmation adapted from Psalm 62.

"For God alone my soul waits in silence.
   My hope comes from God.
   My salvation comes from God.
My mighty rock, my refuge is from God."

Session 5

Whose Body Is This?

Carol Miller

FOCUS This session will help young adults understand that their bodies are created by God for God's purposes and that God supports us as we care for our bodies.

◄ GATHERING ──

Greet one another. Read aloud the following Scripture. "You are not your own.... For you were bought with a price; therefore glorify God in your body" (1 Corinthians 6:19-20). What does this Scripture say to you? What does the phrase "glorify God in your body" say to you? Make a group list of ways to "glorify God" with our bodies.

Pray together the following prayer:
"Loving God, we know we are your creation. Help us to value ourselves and one another as you value us; in Christ we pray. Amen."

Our Bodies Belong to God

Our bodies, as with everything else in creation, were made to bring honor and glory to God. Our bodies belong to God in two important ways: (1) God is the creator of our bodies; (2) our bodies have been redeemed for God's use by Jesus Christ's sacrificial death.

Our bodies, and indeed our whole selves, have been set apart to do God's will. Therefore, misuse of our bodies works against God's will.

Many young adults unintentionally abuse their bodies with over-work, lack of sleep, and lack of exercise. Some young adults may also abuse their bodies because they suffer from a lack of self-esteem, even a subtle self-hatred. We see this form of abuse often in the misuse of drugs, alcohol, tobacco, and food. We also see it in sexual promiscuity.

This session will help you focus your thinking on God's will for your body.

Everyday Miracle

"Toss a precious object into the air and catch it. Now consider the extraordinary device (you, yourself) that just accomplished this everyday miracle. You sensed the energy of the toss, knew the value and importance of success. You triangulated the position of the object throughout its flight with your binocular vision, you edited out distractions by other senses that might divert your attention, you brought an extraordinary signal mechanism into precise operation that triggered one set of muscles after another into a sequence of ground-to-air missile direction-control processes, resulting in easy success as you caught the object without thinking.

"What you did will not make headlines anywhere. It is the simplest example I can think of, of what you do millions of times a day. But ask your friend who knows microelectronics best what it would cost, and how much space it would take, to achieve artificially what you just achieved naturally. He will admit that the problem of reconstituting these simplest excellences of yours would require a major federal grant. But that's just for the easy part.

"Remember that all the miraculous abilities you demonstrated can be naturally and automatically packaged, and preserved without the slightest impairment, for periods of twenty to fifty years or so, in an ultramicroscopic part of you, received by you at no cost and forwarded into the future at the same price, in a tiny segment of a gene in chromosome in a solution so concentrated

that a single teaspoon could contain all the instructions needed to build and operate the three billion people now on the planet."
(From the Forward by David Brower to *Summer Island: Penobscot Country*, by Eliot Porter, edited by David Brower; Sierra Club, 1966)

Dwelling Place for the Holy Spirit

1 Corinthians 3:16-17; 6:12-20. According to the apostle Paul, the bodies of Christians, individually and collectively, are the dwelling places of the Holy Spirit. God has chosen to work in us and through us, to be present in us, to make us instruments to do God's will and work. Therefore our bodies are holy, to be used for God's purposes.

Take out of your purse or pockets either an object of value or something breakable. Toss the object into the air and catch it. How do you usually treat something of value? Why? What other examples can you think of to illustrate the miracle of the human body? Do those examples suggest anything about how we as Christians should treat our bodies? If so, what do they suggest?

The word *holy* means "set apart for God's use." Paul elsewhere called the community of faith the "body of Christ" because the Holy Spirit dwells in the community and gives each individual member skills that serve the whole. In 1 Corinthians 6:12-20 in particular, Paul spoke of the individual Christian as the dwelling place of the Holy Spirit.

Our bodies are not our own; we are not our own. We are vessels for God's Spirit. We live, according to Paul, to serve the One who purchased us with a price, that price being his own suffering and death. A Christian then cannot say, "It's my body, I can do with it what I want." We are stewards of our bodies so we will be able to serve God to the fullest.

A basic belief of Christianity is that Jesus Christ does not want some of our devotion, some of our time, or a bit of our loyalty. Jesus Christ wants us totally. Paul did not recognize the existence of human autonomy, human freedom apart from all authority. Paul contended that we are slaves to whatever we obey

Session 5: Whose Body Is This?

> What does it mean to you to say that belonging "to God in Christ produces life"? What connections do you make between this statement and care for our bodies?

(Romans 6:16). Either we are slaves to sin, "which leads to death," or to obedience to God, which leads to life and increasing holiness (6:17-18).

To belong to God in Christ produces life. When we belong to God—body and soul—we are dedicated to God's will, and we receive life. For our bodies to be set apart for God's use, then, is to be truly alive.

In 1 Corinthians 3, Paul was primarily concerned about contentious persons endangering the wholeness of the Corinthian congregation, which he understood as the body of Christ. In 1 Corinthians 6, Paul shifted his attention to warning those persons who threatened the sanctity of their own bodies with sexual immorality. Paul had taught that the types of food one ate were matters of religious and moral indifference. The fact that food might have been sacrificed to a pagan god—as most meat eaten in Greek cities was—should not prevent Christians from eating it as long as the faith of other, weaker Christians was not threatened. Apparently, some people tried to apply the same logic to their sexual practices. They thought that what they did with their physical bodies, including satisfying sexual desire with prostitutes, was a matter of religious and moral indifference. Paul stated that what one did with one's body very much concerned God.

Read 1 Corinthians 6:19-20. In the following space, write a paraphrase of the Scripture. How does glorifying God in your body compare with loving yourself?

Faith Matters for Young Adults: Living the Faith

The Rhythm of Life

Ecclesiastes 3:1-9 reflects on the rhythm of life. What is right and necessary at one time may be completely out of place at another time. Life has a rhythm, like breathing in and out, that needs to be respected. Life, when lived rightly, is never a constant pushing or a constant pulling. Life includes a time for activity and a time for rest, a time to step forward and a time to step back.

This rhythm in Ecclesiastes concerns human behavior; but the same rhythm of birth and death, activity and rest can be seen in the whole created order. Workaholics and many other people miss this rhythm that renews life and gives order.

Form teams of two or three. Compare your outlines of a typical day. Where do the outlines show a rhythm of working and resting? Do they show a balance of work and rest? Where do they show the stress of constantly needing to do more than is possible?

The Bible does not order us to work and strive constantly without rest. On the contrary, the Old Testament emphasizes the concept of sabbath, instituted by God in Creation and spelled out in the Ten Commandments (Exodus 20:8-11). And nowhere in the Gospel accounts do we see Jesus, who came to save the world, rushing about in a hurry. For example, in Mark 6:30-32 Jesus told his disciples to come away and rest.

Write in the space below an outline of a typical day in your life.

Form teams of two or three persons. As a team make a list of the five most important things persons can do to help their bodies be at their best. Rank the items on your list in order of importance. Compare the list with those of other teams. Try to agree on which items should be ranked as the top three. How well do you follow these directives in your own daily lives? If you do not care for your body well, what reasons can you think of that prevent you from doing so?

How do you know what kind of rhythm life should have? What disrupts the rhythm of life? How do you know that a disruption is not a part of the rhythm? Obviously, things like illness or unexpected events can disrupt life's rhythms. Anything that interferes with the body's health and well being can be seen as disruptive. List some of these things:

Love Others as We Love Ourselves

Matthew 22:39 contains what Jesus called the second greatest commandment. It is originally found in Leviticus 19:18. This Scripture says nothing about loving others instead of ourselves. Jesus commanded his followers to love others in the same way they loved themselves. Rather, our love for ourselves, the kind of constant concern and good will that we have, becomes the pattern for how we love others. So, how do emotionally healthy persons love themselves? Read Matthew 22:34-40. List as many examples as you can to describe what Jesus meant when he said that we should love ourselves.

Improve Your Self-Care

All of us can make choices to improve specific aspects of caring for our bodies. We can decide to rest adequately, to eat balanced diets, to exercise more, and to avoid things that harm our bodies, such as smoking or abuse of alcohol or other drugs. Choose one area to work on during the next few weeks. What can you do in

Faith Matters for Young Adults: Living the Faith

the weeks ahead to care for your body? Choose one thing. Do this one thing until it becomes a habit and a part of the daily rhythm of your life. Write about it below.

— CLOSING WORSHIP —

God Supports You

Any decision you make about caring for your body has God's full support. Whether the thing you want to change is easy or difficult, you can count on God to be with you and to give you the commitment you may need. Caring for our bodies brings honor and glory to God.

Become comfortable in your seat and close your eyes. Spend the next several minutes in silence, sensing your body from the inside. Become aware of different parts of your body and try to feel from the inside. After a couple minutes, open your eyes. Draw, write about, or talk about what you felt your body to be like from the inside.

Close this session with a prayer of thanksgiving for the marvel that is the human body. Ask for God's help in using our bodies for God's glory.

Session 6

Should I Drink? Smoke?

Carol Miller

FOCUS This session guides young adults in making informed decisions about their use of alcohol and tobacco.

– GATHERING –

Greet one another. Upon arrival, write on a large sheet of paper or a chalkboard one question you have about drinking or smoking. When everyone has written a question, review them in the large group.

Pray together the following prayer:
"God of all creation, lead us as we explore the use and abuse of alcohol and tobacco. Show us ways to make good decisions about our use; in Christ we pray. Amen."

Why Drink or Smoke?

This session deals specifically with the use of alcohol and tobacco. What reasons, excuses, or rationales do you offer if you use either alcohol or tobacco? Be honest with yourself.

Christians have varying ideas about their use of alcohol or tobacco. However, biblical principles regarding God's care for all creation are helpful as we consider our use of these substances. It is pointless and unfair to judge a person's character, the state of a person's soul, or a person's moral worth based solely on their use or abuse of alcohol or tobacco. Uncovering our rationalizations and excuses is more helpful. We often offer excuses as we try to avoid doing something we know we need to do. Excuses frequently accompany the use of alcohol and tobacco. Being honest about why we do the things we do will aid people in making objective, well-thought-out decisions.

Use and Abuse of Alcohol

Alcohol is a drug. It has specific effects, some of which are beneficial. Used in excess, however, alcohol is harmful. It is also addictive. Its effects depend on a number of factors such as how much one drinks and one's age. Studies have shown that moderate use (one drink for women and two drinks for men) has beneficial effects on the level of good cholesterol in the bloodstream and on insulin interaction. Excessive use (three drinks at one time for women and four drinks at one time for men) leads to serious problems such as liver disease, high blood pressure, high blood fats (triglycerides), heart failure, stroke, fetal alcohol syndrome, cancer, injury, violence, and death. Alcohol should not be used by pregnant women, children and adolescents, people with family histories of alcohol abuse, and persons taking medications that interact with alcohol.

Many people use alcohol in ways they consider to be harmless, and perhaps, helpful. They use it to
–loosen up in social situations,
–be accepted by the group,
–be sociable,
–relax after a hard day, or
–feel better.

What would you add to this list? What ways, other than drinking alcohol, would help people achieve each reason on the list?

Those who abuse alcohol often become addicted to it. Its main attraction for too many people is its ability to allow them to avoid—temporarily—dealing with difficult or unpleasant situations such as:
–facing their anger
–facing feelings of inadequacy
–facing disappointments
–dealing with relationships
–facing problems
–facing fears
–facing pain

What would you add to this list? What ways, other than drinking alcohol, would help people with the difficult situations on the list?

Session 6: Should I Drink? Smoke?   51

The Excuse

The following paragraph written by Jack London illustrates excuses or rationalizations for excessive use of alcohol. It points to the lack of control that often signals alcoholism.

"I was perpetually finding excuses for extra cocktails. It might be the assembling of a particularly jolly crowd; a touch of anger against my architect or against a thieving stonemason working on my barn; the death of my favorite horse in a barbed wire fence; or news of good fortune in the morning mail from my dealings with editors and publishers. It was immaterial what the excuse might be, once the desire had germinated in me."

Jack London

Read aloud "The Excuse." What is your response to London's description? How can his words be helpful with your choice about whether or not to have a drink?

Smoke Screen

The Center for Disease Control, a division of the United States Department of Health and Human Services, reports "adverse health effects from cigarette smoking account for 440,000 deaths, or nearly 1 of every 5 deaths, each year in the United States. More deaths are caused each year by tobacco use than by all deaths from human immunodeficiency virus (HIV), illegal drug use, alcohol use, motor vehicle injuries, suicides, and murders combined." Smoking has been shown to cause cancer, cardiovascular diseases, and respiratory diseases. Smoking and other forms of tobacco use are addictive.

What is your response to the statistics from the Center for Disease Control? How do such statistics measure into a choice to smoke or not to smoke?

In spite of the fact that both smoking and breathing secondhand smoke have been proven to have harmful effects, some people choose to smoke. Read some of the reasons and rationalizations for smoking in the following list. In the space provided, write a response to each one.

1. Smoking is just a habit.

2. Smoking relaxes me.

3. I smoke because I like the taste of tobacco.

4. My grandfather started smoking when he was twelve, and he lived to be eighty-eight.

5. I'm not addicted; I can quit any-time I want to.

What other reasons or rationalizations for smoking have you heard?

6. It's my body; smoking is my business.

We can respond to each of these reasons or rationalizations for smoking in a variety of ways. Some possible responses might include the following: (1) Habits can be broken. (2) Other ways to relax do not put us at risk for diseases. (3) Is the taste of tobacco worth risking your health for? (4) "My grandfather . . ." is simply playing with statistical probability. The probability that applies is that the more one smokes the greater the probability of health problems. (5) Nicotine is physically addictive, and the psychological dependence on smoking is also a kind of addiction. (6) As a Christian, one cannot use this excuse. Our bodies are God's to be used for God. In addition, our poor health hurts those who love us. Secondhand smoke causes harm to other people. Our poor example may encourage others, including children, to take up this health-risking habit.

What Does the Bible Say?

Proverbs 23:29-35 offers a view from 2,500 years ago of a person who has had too much to drink. A tragic situation sounds almost (though not quite) humorous. The Scripture lists some of the problems the person encounters as a result of his drinking (23:29). It describes the effects of drunkenness and the hangover (23:32-33), which the person intends to cure with another drink, just to wake up (23:35). This Old Testament Scripture helps us see that getting drunk is nothing new, nor is it clever or on the cutting edge of social behavior. Drunkenness and alcoholism have been around as long as alcohol itself.

Read Proverbs 23:29-35 in several different versions of the Bible. What does this Scripture say to you about the plight of one who drinks too much? How can it inform your choices about drinking?

In Romans 14:13-23 Paul discussed whether a Christian should eat the meat sold in the marketplace, knowing that it had been offered as a sacrifice in pagan worship to idols. Paul contended that idols have no power, so eating meat offered to idols was not a problem. However, persons whose faith is weak might see you eating such meat and think that you approve of idol worship. Those persons might then be tempted to worship idols. If that is the case, then the one strong in faith should refrain from eating meat dedicated to idols so as not to tempt anyone else inadvertently. Your action may not be wrong for you; but if it might cause someone else to stumble, then you must refrain from that action out of love for the other person.

The Christian's main concern is the welfare of others. Christians do not use their freedom in Christ to hurt others. The key to

Christian decision making is Romans 14:21. Paul repeated this warning in 1 Corinthians 6:12-14; 10:23-33.

What Does Your Church Say?

Many churches or denominations have statements about the use and abuse of alcohol and tobacco. The Social Principles of The United Methodist Church, for example, contain these statements: "We affirm our long-standing support of abstinence from alcohol as a faithful witness to God's liberating and redeeming love for persons." As the use of alcohol is "a major factor in both disease and death . . . , we support educational programs. . . encouraging abstinence" from such use; and "in light of the overwhelming evidence that tobacco smoking and the use of smokeless tobacco are hazardous to the health of persons of all ages, we recommend total abstinence from the use of tobacco . . . and support the restriction of smoking in public areas and workplaces." Your denomination may have similar statements.

Reading such statements can add another helpful resource to your decisions about drinking and smoking.

How might this Scripture inform your choices about smoking or drinking? How might others in your life experience be harmed from your choices? What would be the benefits for them if you choose not to drink or not to smoke?

The Strength of Christ

"I can do all things through him who strengthens me" (Philippians 4:13). Many persons struggling against addictions have found Paul's words to be a source of great power. We should keep in mind, however, that Paul wrote this verse within the community of faith. He was not talking about lone individuals. Paul always knew that much of the strength of God's Holy Spirit was mediated to him through the community of faith. Anyone dealing with addictions needs the love and support of the Christian community.

Form two teams. Team 1 make a list of all the reasons for abstaining from the use of alcohol or tobacco. Team 2 make a list of all the reasons for moderation in the use of alcohol or tobacco. Talk about the lists with the entire group.

Such love and support offered in the name of Christ can help persons "do all things."

▬ CLOSING WORSHIP ▬

Read aloud Philippians 4:13. Offer sentence prayers for strength to make right decisions and for strength to break bad habits.

Session 7

How Can My Behaviors Harm Me?

Carol Miller

FOCUS This session will explore what Christian faith has to offer to those who are dealing with issues related to drug abuse and eating disorders. It will help young adults make informed decisions about the use and abuse of drugs and about their eating habits.

— GATHERING —

Greet one another. Look at pictures from current magazines that show people of varying weights and sizes, in varying socio-economic settings, and doing varying activities involving work, family, recreation, parties, and so forth. Write on a piece of paper your first impressions of the people in the pictures. Do you think some of the people in the pictures look more intelligent or more successful than others? If so, why? Which ones might abuse drugs? Which ones might suffer from an eating disorder? What role does physical appearance play in your judgments? In what ways did a person's body size or apparent socio-economic group make a difference in your first impressions? How does the activity pictured influence your judgment?

Pray together the following prayer:
"God of all people, help us to see people as you do. Help us to remember that you love and value all humans no matter what. Guide us as we explore the issues of drug abuse and overeating. Help us to hear what we need to hear in order to make good decisions in these areas of our lives. Amen."

All Humans Are Valued by God

This session deals with two potentially self-destructive activities—drug abuse and harmful eating habits, both of which are problems about which people make choices. Severe drug addiction and eating disorders such as bulimia and anorexia nervosa are beyond the reach of this session. We will look at what our Christian faith says about the worth of all persons and what it has to offer as we make choices about drugs and about eating.

> What other distorted or uninformed perceptions might lead to a person's decision to use drugs or engage in harmful eating habits?

At first glance, one might wonder what drug abuse and eating disorders have in common. Drug abuse is almost universally agreed to be among the gravest problems that American society faces today. News reports every day include stories about lives ruined and ended because of drug abuse. Violence and corruption sweep large and small cities as criminals seek the profits that come from the enormous network of illicit drug trade.

But what about eating disorders? How many people would consider eating disorders to be a problem of the same magnitude as drug abuse? Yet both drug abuse and eating disorders, like alcohol abuse and the use of tobacco, frequently have their roots in distorted perceptions such as self-hatred, low self-esteem, or lack of adequate understanding about what one can or cannot control.

All human beings are persons of worth and deserve respect and compassion. We know this truth because of the love that Jesus Christ gives us. We are the ones "for whom Christ died" (Romans 14:15). Our worth as human beings does not come from anything we have accomplished or from any choices, good or bad, that we make. Our worth derives solely in the fact that Christ died for us. No human being is worthless.

God Offers Hope

Another major issue related to drug abuse and eating disorders is a feeling of hopelessness. This too can be deep-rooted. While most of us are not professionals who are qualified to help people deal with the intricacies of self-abuse, as Christians we can offer two truths that can help persons with these complicated problems. These two truths can help us as well when we need to make choices about drugs and eating.

No one needs to live without hope. First, the resurrection of Jesus Christ from the dead means much more than life with God after death. It means the possibility of new life in this world and this time. Second, God is always with us. We can lay foundations for both recovery and for life-giving choices as we claim for ourselves the personal worth and the hope present in the powerful love of Jesus Christ.

> How do you think God offers hope for those plagued with drug abuse, either their own or that of a family member or a friend? How do you think God offers hope to persons who abuse their bodies through overeating or who suffer from eating disorders such as anorexia or bulimia? How does God offer hope to us as we make choices about drugs and eating?

Weight . . . It's Not Always a Problem

People who are overweight are not necessarily abusing their bodies with food. A number of medical conditions can cause persons to be overweight (or underweight). Also, some studies have shown that it may be healthier for people to maintain their weight, even if they are overweight, than to lose and gain it back again and again. If a person is overweight but healthy and content with his or her body size, then weight is not a problem. Think about cultural prejudices that are based on appearance. Consider how advertising and media images reinforce such prejudices. List some of your thoughts about cultural prejudices regarding weight in the following space:

> Invite a helping professional who deals with either drug abuse or eating disorders to speak to the group. Have the speaker give basic information about the nature of the problem, how a person realizes that he or she has a problem, and where to go to seek help. Include time for questions to which the speaker responds.

Weight is a problem in some situations. If weight, either over-weight or underweight, creates a serious health risk, or if concern about weight becomes an obsession or leads to severe eating disorders, then weight is a problem. It is a problem if it creates a feeling of self-loathing. In this case, the real problem may be the self-loathing rather than the weight. Anyone who uses weight as an excuse to avoid dealing with relationships or with other issues and challenges in life has a problem. What other situations around weight do you think would indicate a problem?

People who suffer from eating disorders may do so for a number of reasons. The real issues may be the emotions that emerge from other situations in life. Some of these reasons may include
–to feel comfort in times of loneliness or rejection
–to feel loved
–to punish oneself
–to avoid rejection ("it's not me they reject: it's my weight")
–to avoid romantic situations by being unattractive
–anger turned inward

What would you add to the list above? How does our faith help with each of the situations listed? Write about your ideas in the following space:

Drug Abuse Has Medical and Societal Consequences

The National Institute of Drug Abuse reports the following information on its website. "Drug addiction is a brain disease. Although initial drug use might be voluntary, drugs of abuse have been shown to alter gene expression and brain circuitry, which in turn affect human behavior. Once addiction develops, these brain changes interfere with an individual's ability to make voluntary decisions, leading to compulsive drug craving, seeking and use. The impact of addiction can be far reaching. Cardiovascular disease, stroke, cancer, HIV/AIDS, hepatitis, and lung disease can all be affected by drug abuse. Some of these effects occur when drugs are used at high doses or after prolonged use, however, some may occur after just one use." (*www.nida.nih.gov/consequences*)

> What insights do you gain from the information about the effects of drug use and addiction? How do these insights affect your choices about use of drugs?

NIDA also cites a 1992 study about the costs of drug abuse that estimated the total economic cost of alcohol and drug abuse to be $245.7 billion. "Of this cost, $97.7 billion was due to drug abuse. This estimate includes substance abuse treatment and prevention costs as well as other healthcare costs, costs associated with reduced job productivity or lost earnings, and other costs to society such as crime and social welfare." Such costs are staggering. They illustrate the immensity of the problem. Yet, the real tragedy of drug abuse rests in the often unquantifiable emotional, physical, mental, and spiritual consequences for the person who abuses drugs and for that person's family and friends.

> What emotional, physical, mental, and spiritual consequences would you identify for the families and friends of those who abuse drugs? How does Christian faith address the concerns of families and friends?

People choose to abuse drugs for a number of reasons. Many think that they have the self-control to use drugs recreationally and to avoid addiction. They tell themselves, "I can handle it."

Many want to have fun or to experience the feelings caused by drugs. This is often the case with celebrities and cultural icons who become addicted or who have died as a result of drug abuse. It is also true that some persons use drugs in order to be accepted by others, to avoid or dull either physical or emotional pain, to relieve the stress of daily problems, or to punish themselves either consciously or unconsciously. People who become addicted often continue a family pattern of addiction.

> What Christian belief or ideal seems most appropriate to you for persons who abuse drugs? What would offer hope? What Christian belief best informs your choices regarding drugs?

How Can the Bible Help?

Exodus 16:13-21. When the Hebrews escaped from slavery in Egypt, they spent years wandering in the wilderness. Early in their wanderings, they ran out of food. Many of the Israelites complained that they should have remained in slavery. At least when they were slaves in Egypt, they never starved.

Exodus 16:13-21 presents the story of God's response to the hunger of the Israelites. God provided manna and quails for their food. But notice that God only provided exactly enough to satisfy hunger.

> How might Exodus 16:13-21 help you as you make choices regarding food or drugs?

The point of the story is that the people needed to learn to trust God. God provides the necessities for life. When the Hebrews stored more manna than they needed for the day, God caused it to rot. Fear, uncertainty, and doubt are enemies of the trust one should have in God.

Trust in God can help people make good choices about eating or about the use of drugs. We sometimes feel the desire to lean on other things to insure our mental or physical well being. Think about the types of things in which you or your group place your trust. List responses in the following space:

Matthew 6:25-33 is part of Jesus' Sermon on the Mount (Matthew 5–7). He directed these words to the crowds of people who followed him and to his followers. In this Scripture Jesus described the basic attitude that Christians should hold toward life. Christians put their whole trust in God.

How might Matthew 6:25-33 help you as you make choices regarding food or drugs?

Jesus' message is to give our worry to God and to trust God's love for us. Jesus tells us to put doing God's will first. The necessities of life will follow from that.

Ephesians 2:4-10 provides one of the most magnificent statements of the sure hope that is ours in Jesus Christ. God has loved us when we were unlovable. God has saved us when we did not deserve salvation. God has recreated us in Jesus Christ to do God's will. Without any reference to who we are, what our background is, or what we have or have not done, God has saved us. This session includes this message of hope directed to those who feel hopeless and worthless.

Form two teams. Team 1 deal with the issue of drug addiction and abuse. Team 2 deal with issues related to harmful eating habits. Read Exodus 16:13-21; Matthew 6:25-33; and Ephesians 2:4-10. What hope do these Scriptures offer to those who abuse drugs? To those who struggle with issues related to weight or eating disorders?

CLOSING WORSHIP

Pray for all persons who are dealing with addiction or eating disorders. Pray for guidance in making your own choices about eating and about using drugs. Close the session with the Lord's Prayer.

Session 8

How May Christians View Intimacy and Sexuality?

Pamela Dilmore

FOCUS This session will help young adults examine a Christian and biblical understanding of themselves as sexual and sensual persons and of the meaning of intimacy.

- GATHERING ——

Ahead of time write the words "sex" and "Christian" on a large sheet of paper or a chalkboard and post this in an easily accessible location. Write a phrase or sentence that tells something about your feelings or thoughts about a Christian view of sex. Review the sentences and phrases in the entire group.

Read aloud: "So God created humankind in his image, / in the image of God he created them; / male and female he created them" (Genesis 1:27).

Pray together the following prayer:
"God of all creation, guide us as we explore human sexuality, sensuality, and intimacy. Help us as we reflect upon Christian choices in these areas of our lives; in Christ we pray. Amen."

Cultural Views

Our culture is saturated with images associated with human sexuality, intimacy, and sensuality. Music, plays, television, movies, magazines, and newspapers entice us with images of women and men who represent flawless, idealized projections of attractiveness. Society leads us to believe that happiness results from our ability to attract and seduce the opposite sex. These images seem to say that a human relationship must include sexual intercourse if it is to be intimate and meaningful.

In our culture young adults struggle as they seek guidance for choices about intimacy and sexuality from Christian tradition and from the Bible. The world around them and the world of the Bible seem far apart. Being a Christian does not mean that a young adult is not a sexual being. All human beings are

> Discuss group responses to the questions in this section. What other questions do you have?

sexual. How should a Christian make choices about sexuality and intimacy in a society that glamorizes and idealizes sexual attractiveness? How can we find God's will regarding sexual behavior when today's world and the biblical world seem so different? What does the Bible say about sexuality and intimacy? In the following space respond to one or more of these questions.

Case Studies

Read and discuss the following case studies with your group as time allows. Write your responses to the questions in the spaces provided after each case study.

Tanya is a single Christian woman strongly attracted to someone at work who is also single. She feels guilty about her sexual feelings. She asks herself, *Are my feelings wrong?* What do you think? Are they? Why or why not?

Fred and Carrie are good friends. Both enjoy running. They run together every Saturday morning to prepare for their day. They often have breakfast together afterward. Should their relationship include sexual intercourse? Why or why not?

Ron and Linda are engaged. Both are active in church. They teach a children's Sunday school class together and sing in the choir. They plan to marry when they finish college in two more years. What kinds of sexual behavior are appropriate for them, if any? Is it all right for them to have sexual intercourse? Why or why not?

John is an athletic, handsome young man who dates often. He has not experienced sexual intercourse and feels embarrassed to tell anyone. He has been led to believe that men should be experienced. He worries about AIDS and other sexually transmitted diseases. He does not want to father a child outside of marriage. He feels that sexual intercourse should be an expression of a committed and caring relationship. Right now he is dating one young woman steadily. They are sexually attracted to one another. Should they have sexual intercourse? Why or why not?

Sexuality, Sensuality, and Intimacy

The terms *sexuality, intimacy,* and *sensuality* are often confused. Look at the triangle that follows. Brainstorm words, definitions, or ideas associated with each term. Write these words near *sexual-*

ity, sensuality, or *intimacy* inside the triangle on their student page. If your word seems to fit more than one of these terms, then place it in the area between the words. As you write each response, ask these questions: Could this response also fit in another corner of the triangle? If so, why? Where do you think it fits best? Why?

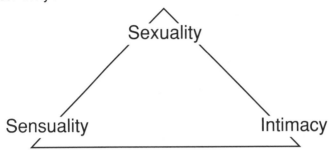

Sexuality

Sensuality   Intimacy

Intimacy, or *intimate* has a range of meanings. *Intimate* can mean the inmost nature or character of someone or something. It is often used to refer to something familiar, close, or private. When used to describe knowledge, it refers to a knowledge that comes from close study. Intimacy can describe an atmosphere that produces a feeling of privacy, coziness, or romance. It can also refer to sexual intercourse.

Sensuality refers to the body or the senses. A sensual person is one who enjoys the stimulation of the physical senses or who is preoccupied with bodily and sexual pleasure.

"Sexuality is the fullness of who we are as embodied male and female persons. Sensuality is the capacity for experience and expression through the senses. Intimacy occurs in an interpersonal relationship characterized by mutuality, the ability to know and be known. In an intimate relationship a person experiences change without losing the unique sense of self." (Dr. Judith Orr, formerly assistant professor of pastoral care and counseling and academic dean, Saint Paul School of Theology)

Sexuality refers to all that is associated with sex; the sexes; the organs of sex; and the behaviors, drives, and instincts associated with sex. It is often used to describe behaviors associated with male and female roles. All human beings are "sexual" persons.

Sexuality, sensuality, and intimacy may or may not include the activities involved in physical sexual pleasure and sexual intercourse. The need for physical sexual pleasure is a God-given part of our existence as human beings. It is a part of who we are, but it is not all of who we are.

What Does the Bible Say?

Genesis 2:18-25. God recognizes that it is good for Adam to be in relationship with another human. Relationships enhance and encourage human wholeness and well-being. The word *helper* suggests this relationship will be characterized by mutual interdependence.

The creation of the woman from the man's rib expresses the deep communion between the two humans. The man recognizes this communion and expresses it in the joyful cry of 2:23. Sex is not regarded as evil. It is blessed by God. The man and the woman are not ashamed of their nakedness. Their relationship to each other and to God carries no guilt.

Read Genesis 2:18-25 and write responses to the following questions:

What does God say about the aloneness of the man? In what ways does God deal with the aloneness?

What do you think the man means when he says "bone of my bones and flesh of my flesh" (2:23)?

How do you think the man feels when he sees the woman? Why?

What attitude is expressed about sexual intercourse in 2:24?

What is the attitude toward nakedness in 2:25?

What does this story say to you about human sexuality?

Song of Solomon 5:10-16. In this Scripture, the "fairest among women" (1:8) describes her "beloved" (5:10). His physical charms are not regarded as evil. Instead she praises him with glowing poetry that places the physical in the realm of beauty.

She refers to the man she loves as "beloved" in 5:10, 16. She also refers to him as "friend" in 5:16. These references imply that her relationship to him includes spiritual connectedness as well as physical attraction.

Read Song of Solomon 5:10-16. Write responses to the following questions:

What names does the woman give to the one she loves? What do these names tell you about her relationship to him?

What are these verses describing? What kinds of descriptions do they use? What do these descriptions tell you about the woman's feelings?

What do these verses say to you about human sexuality?

Song of Solomon 7:1-9. The man in this Scripture describes the woman, praising her physical charms in glowing poetic language. He refers to her as "queenly maiden" (7:1) and "loved one, delectable maiden" (7:6). "Queenly" carries with it a sense of respect (7:1). "Loved one" indicates his spiritual connection to her. "Delectable" reveals his desire for her. All these qualities of relationship are combined as he describes her physical charms and reveals his passion for her.

The way the man and the woman poetically praise each other's physical charms also reveals the spiritual nature of the relationship. Intimacy, sensuality, and sexuality connect in these passages. The church has traditionally viewed Song of Solomon as symbolizing God's relationship with humanity.

Read Song of Solomon 7:1-9. Write responses to the following questions:
What do the names the man gives to the woman tell you about his relationship to her?

Write "Genesis 2:18-25"; "Song of Solomon 5:10-16"; and "Song of Solomon 7:1-9" on index cards. Form three teams. Give each group a card. Each team read the Scripture listed on the card. Discuss the responses to the questions listed in the book for that Scripture. When everyone has finished, each team tell the entire group about the highlights of their discussion. Decide whether the Scripture deals with sexuality, sensuality, or intimacy. Could the Scripture fit with more than one of these terms? Which ones? Why?

What are these verses describing? What kinds of descriptions do they use? What do these descriptions tell you about the man's feelings?

What is your response to Song of Solomon 7:8-9?

What do these verses say to you about human sexuality?

Session 8: How May Christians View Intimacy and Sexuality?   71

The Great Commandment

Mark 12:28-34; Matthew 22:34-40; and Luke 10:25-28 give accounts of the Great Commandment. A scribe approached Jesus and asked him which law is the greatest. Jesus responded with quotations from Deuteronomy 6:5 and Leviticus 19:18, which say to love God with your whole being and to love your neighbor as yourself. The passages list three loves—God, self, and neighbor. Love of God is the basis for love of self and neighbor. The Great Commandment recognizes that our actions do not occur in isolation. They have an impact on others. Making Christian choices involves asking ourselves how our actions will affect loving relationships with God, our self, and our neighbor.

> What does the Great Commandment offer to us? How does it guide us in making Christian choices about sexuality?

The Greek word for *love* in these three passages is *agapao.* This word is more than sentiment or feeling. It includes judgment and the assent of the will. It includes intellect as well as feeling, and it indicates the self-giving love of God.

God's Gift and Human Choice

As we consider God's gifts of sexuality, sensuality, and intimacy, it is good to remember that these gifts can be abused. When we make choices that harm our selves or others, we have ventured away from God's will. Sin can be understood as a distortion of love. When a person chooses to act to gratify a selfish interest without regard for God or neighbor, the action is sin. Actions have consequences, both good and bad. Agape love wills good consequences for God, self, and neighbor. Looking at consequences can help us make Christian choices about human sexuality.

CLOSING WORSHIP —

Stand in a circle and hold hands. Pray the following prayer or one of your own:

"God of all creation, you are truly a loving God. We are ready to open our hearts and our minds to you. We want to know your ways of love. Help us to understand our sexuality as a good gift from you. Help us to express our sexuality in positive and loving ways; in the name of Jesus. Amen."

Session 9

How May Christians View Singleness?

Pamela Dilmore

FOCUS This session will help young adults explore Christian and biblical understandings of singleness and how these understandings can inform singleness in contemporary culture.

- GATHERING —

Ahead of time write the word "singleness" on a large sheet of paper or a chalkboard. Participants draw images that the word suggests. Talk about these images with the entire group.

Pray together the following prayer:
"God of all people, guide us as we explore singleness in the Bible, in churches, and in our culture. Help us to reclaim the truth of your love for all persons, single and married; in Christ we pray. Amen."

Caring Attitudes Toward Single Persons

Our culture often regards singleness as a less desirable status than marriage. Our churches often reinforce this attitude by providing programs geared primarily to meet the needs of married people and of families with children. A healthy, caring congregation that seeks to be a nurturing community will meet the concerns, needs, and joys of single persons by making a place for them in their existing ministries and by offering programs designed to meet their specific needs.

A Singleness Crossword Puzzle

Below you will find the beginnings of a crossword puzzle based on the word *singleness.* Think of words that you associate with singleness. Add your words to the crossword puzzle at available locations.

Share the words you have added to the crossword puzzle with the entire group. In what way do you associate these words with singleness? How do they make you think of singleness in positive ways? in negative ways? In what ways might our culture associate these words with singleness? In what ways might our churches associate these words with singleness? In what ways might our families associate these words with singleness?

```
            C
            O
            M
            P O W E R
            L   H
      A L O N E   O     J
            T   L     E
    S I NG L EN E S   S
                U
                S
```

Case Studies

Persons who are single vary in age, gender, and interests just as people who are not single vary. Below are case studies of four single persons. Jim and Leslie are single persons who have never been married. Mark and Margo are single again. They have known what it is like to be married. As you read about these four single persons, consider their differences as well as what they might have in common.

JIM: I'm really glad to be back in school! I am a graduate student, and I just had the most frustrating Christmas you can imagine.

My parents think I want to stay in school forever—you know, be a career student. More than that, they think I ought to be married. I'm their only child, you see, and they want grandchildren. Do parents ever let up? They are driving my girlfriend and me nuts.

MARGO: My husband died of cancer five years ago. For the first three years after his death, I didn't know if I would make it through the grief. I still miss him. I don't have any children, and I sometimes feel lonely. But in the past few months I have really begun to appreciate the settled rhythm of my life. I enjoy being in charge of my own schedule and not having to check with anyone. My friends keep trying to match me up with single men. They say I'm too young to be single. I'm not sure I want to date right now. I think I like being single.

Four group members choose a case study, one case study per member. Read the case study aloud. Feel free to roleplay or to develop a skit based the case studies. Answer the questions after the readings. Discuss your responses with the entire group.

LESLIE: My job is fun, and I like the people I work with, but—I don't know—it's just not enough. I have always wanted a home and family to care for. I'd like to meet someone, fall in love, and get married. I'd feel happy and fulfilled if I had a family.

MARK: I came from a large family. We were close, and I always knew I wanted the same large family one day. Things didn't work out the way I planned. I was divorced a year ago. My former wife and son live four hours away. Every other week, I drive the distance so I can spend time with my son.

Read the following questions and write responses in the spaces provided.

In what ways might their lives as single persons be similar?

In what ways are their lives as single persons different?

Describe what you think each person might feel about being single.

In what ways might each person's expectations about the future be different? the same?

In what ways might the church meet the needs of each of these single persons?

The Bible and Singleness

The Hebrew society out of which the Bible emerged valued the family as its basic unit. Individuals found their worth according to their role within the family. The father was the head of the family. His wives, children, and slaves were thought of as his property. Singleness presented problems in such a system. As a general rule, single people lived on the edge of society in Bible times. But we also find a few stories in the Bible about single people who lived fruitful lives in a family-oriented culture.

Luke 2:36-38. The story of Anna tells about a Jewish woman who was a widow and a prophet. She spent her days fasting and praying in the Temple. Most Jewish women looked to marriage and children as their lifetime goal. If they did not marry, they had few options for survival other than remaining with their original family. Anna's husband died after seven years of marriage. Like Simeon in 2:25-35, Anna looked for the Messiah to bring the reign of God.

> Read Luke 2:36–38. In what ways do you see Anna living a fruitful life? Do you think she should have chosen a different lifestyle? Why or why not? Do you know anyone like Anna? If so, tell about her.

Both Anna and Simeon were at the Temple when Joseph and Mary arrived after the birth of Jesus for the rites of purification after childbirth and the redemption of the firstborn. Simeon, an aged prophet who had been promised by God that he would see the Messiah before he died, saw the hope of the Messiah fulfilled in Jesus. He declared that in the infant Jesus, salvation and glory had come into the world, both for Israel and for the Gentiles.

> Read 1 Corinthians 7:17–35. List advantages and disadvantages of being married according to Paul. List advantages and disadvantages of singleness according to Paul. Do you agree or disagree with Paul's ideas? Why?

Anna was the second witness in the Temple. Like Simeon, she gave thanks to God for the hope of redemption fulfilled in the child.

1 Corinthians 7:8-40. In 1 Corinthians 7:8 we learn that the apostle Paul was single. He told the church in Corinth that either singleness or marriage is acceptable (7:17, 25-35). In either state one should lead the life to which one is called. But in 7:25-40 Paul clearly favors singleness, an unusual position in a culture that placed high value on the family. Christians in Paul's day believed the Lord would return during their lifetime. This belief colored Paul's attitudes. Although he did not consider marriage sinful, he viewed it as distracting: "I want you to be free from anxieties" (7:32).

Men and women experience divided interests when they are married. Husbands and wives are anxious about worldly affairs and about how to please their spouses. Paul preferred singleness because he saw it as a condition in which persons could give all devotion to the Lord. This passage offers a positive view of singleness in a culture that valued marriage and family as the basic institutions.

Advantages and Disadvantages

Anyone can make a case for either marriage or singleness by focusing on advantages and disadvantages of each. List the advantages and disadvantages of singleness in the following space.

Advantages

Disadvantages

On a large sheet of paper or a chalkboard, write the words "Advantages" and "Disadvantages" at the tops of two columns. Form two teams. Team 1 list advantages of singleness. Team 2 list disadvantages of singleness. Have someone from each group report the list to the entire group. List the group's results in the appropriate columns on the paper or chalkboard. What other advantages would you add? What other disadvantages? Why? Which advantages or disadvantages in the lists challenge you? Why?

Alone or Lonely?

"I am alone, but I am not lonely." These words make us pause and think. What does it mean to be alone? What does it mean to be lonely? Loneliness and aloneness suggest significant differences in feeling. The poem that follows offers some insights to consider. Read it silently and think about what it says.

Alone or Lonely

To be lonely
    is to need,
    is to feed on another's presence.
Loneliness consumes
    another's presence
    to fill a void,
    to end a pain.
The value of the other depends
    on filling that void,
    attending to that need,
    ending that pain.
The lonely person says,
    "Take away my loneliness!
    Make me happy again!"

To be alone
    is to nourish the self
    that it might grow,
    that it might give.
To be alone
    is to prepare a feast
    as an offering to a friend.
The value of the other depends
    on who they are,
    in their own being and becoming,
    in their aloneness.
To be alone
    is to receive
    the recreating energy
    to love and live.

—PD, 1992

Do you agree or disagree with the poem's description of aloneness? of loneliness? Why? Write your reflections in the following space.

Single or Married, We Are Not Alone

The message of the Bible and Christian faith is that we are not alone. God is with all persons whether married or single. We can be assured that whether we choose marriage or singleness as a way of life, God gives what we need through the presence and power of Christ.

Read aloud the poem "Alone or Lonely." What does being lonely mean to you? What can a person who is feeling lonely do to "fill a void" or "end a pain"? What does being alone mean to you? What are some ways to receive "recreating energy"? What does "prepare a feast" mean to you? In what ways does preparing a feast differ from consuming? Why do you think the poem describes loneliness as consuming?

CLOSING WORSHIP ──

Have the group members pray the following prayer to close the session:

"Loving God, you have shown us through Jesus that you love all human beings, married and single, single and single again. Teach us to believe that we have value. Teach us new ways to accept your love and show our love for you. Teach us to love ourselves better so that we may love others better; in the name of Jesus we pray. Amen."

Session 10

How May Christians View Marriage and Divorce?

Pamela Dilmore

FOCUS This session will help young adults examine a Christian and biblical understanding of marriage and divorce and how these understandings inform marriage and divorce in contemporary culture.

– GATHERING –

Look through old magazines to find pictures or words describing what you expect marriage to be like. Glue these pictures and words onto construction paper to create a collage that expresses your expectations. Ask participants to explain their collages. What is marriage? In what ways are your expectations of marriage similar to those of others in the group? In what ways are they different? When you think about marriage, what do you hope for? What are you afraid of?

Pray together the following prayer or one of your own.
"Caring and loving God, guide us as we consider the making and breaking of our intimate covenants. Reveal to us your ways of love; in Christ we pray. Amen."

Case Studies

The 2000 census reveals that couples are marrying at later ages and that the divorce rate, while not significantly different from the findings for the 1980's, is still near 50 percent. No wonder we have questions about marriage and divorce! What does the covenant of Christian marriage mean in our culture? How does the Christian faith inform a decision to divorce? These questions are challenging, and answers to them are profoundly shaped by our personal and cultural expectations. Some possible reasons for such high rates of divorce are

– Birth control has changed the way people think about the marriage relationship.
– Promises aren't as important as they used to be.
– Divorce is an easy way out when marriage is no longer fun.
– Male and female roles have drastically changed in the past twenty years.
– More people are in hurtful or destructive relationships than twenty years ago.
– Values today are different from those of twenty years ago.
– People today are more concerned with what they get than with what they give.

> Which reasons do you think contribute most to the high rates of divorce? Why? What reasons for divorce would you add to this list?

Some Case Sudies

Read each of the following case studies. What is happening in each situation? Is the relationship healthy or unhealthy? What do you think needs to happen for the benefit of both in each marriage? Is divorce appropriate or inappropriate? Why? Write your reflections in the space provided after each case study.

Miriam is in the hospital. She told the doctor that her black eye and her broken arm happened because she fell down the stairs at home. Her husband, **Fred,** is sitting in the room with her. He has brought her a dozen long-stemmed red roses. He has been crying. He says he loves her and will never hurt her again. Miriam thinks maybe this time he really means it.

Tom and Allie are sitting in front of the television set in their den. Allie is bored. She likes tennis and swimming. Tom enjoys movies and going out to dinner. When they were dating, they seemed to have more in common. After being married for two years, they have discovered that their interests are very different. They were trying to please each other when they were dating. Tom seems content. But for Allie marriage doesn't seem to be fun anymore.

Charles and Katherine are parents of three small children. Both of them work. By the time they get home, the children need attention. They never seem to have enough time to get everything done; and when the day is over, both are too exhausted for conversation or recreation. Recently Charles discovered that Katherine has been seeing an old boyfriend during her lunch hour.

Rose was a successful businesswoman when she met and married **Dan**. He was romantic and showered her with attention until they were married. He seemed proud of her beauty, poise, and intelligence. After they were married, he became increasingly jealous of her contacts with business associates. He tells her that she does not have to work because he makes enough money to support them. Every evening when she gets home, he quizzes her about where she has been and whom she has seen. Recently he has begun to accuse her of being unfaithful. Rose feels angry and smothered. She wonders what happened to that romantic man she married.

Marriage Vows

A covenant is a formal agreement or treaty between two parties with each assuming some obligation. The word *covenant* is used to describe the relationship between God and God's people. In Malachi and Ezekiel it is also used to refer to the marriage relationship. Marriage vows are expressions of a covenant mutually agreed upon by a couple at their wedding. The vows define their relationship.

Look at the following marriage vows:

"In the name of God,
I, *Name,* take you, *Name,* to be my wife (husband),
to have and to hold
from this day forward,
for better, for worse,
for richer, for poorer,
in sickness and in health,
to love and to cherish,
until we are parted by death.
This is my solemn vow."

> Form teams of two or three. Compose an ideal set of marriage vows. Share these vows with the entire group.

(From "A Service of Christian Marriage," *The United Methodist Hymnal,* The United Methodist Publishing House, 1989; page 867)

In the spaces provided write brief responses to the following questions:

What is the purpose of marriage vows?

What vows or promises would you be willing to make in marriage?

What does "for better, for worse" mean to you?

Do you think any "for worse" situation warrants breaking the vows of a marriage? If so, what might such a situation be?

What Does the Bible Say About Marriage and Divorce?

In the times described in the Old Testament, the well being of the group was more important than the well being of the individual. James Efird in *What the Bible Says* (Abingdon, 1985; page 19) states that survival was tied to the well being of the group. The good of the group was often pursued at the expense of an individual's life. The basic group was the family with a male at its head. All family members and servants were considered his property. Marriage and divorce customs in the Old Testament should be understood against this background.

Marriage. In biblical times, marriage was arranged or consented to by parents. The groom paid a "bride price" to the family of the bride, who was considered her father's property. After a period of betrothal, the bride was moved from her father's house to the house of the groom, where she became her husband's property. Faithfulness in marriage was the ideal. Adultery was counted as a sin against one's neighbor and against

> How do you respond to the view that the bride is the "property" of the groom?

God. It was a violation both of purity laws and of the laws protecting property.

Ephesians 5:21-33 discusses marriage. Ephesians 5:21 tells married persons, "Be subject to one another out of reverence for Christ." This verse is a powerful lens for viewing the verses that follow. It reshapes centuries of tradition with a simple and profound statement of equality based on reverence of Christ. New Testament society was patriarchal. The husband

> Read Ephesians 5:21-23 and Acts 18:1-4, 18, 24-26. In what ways are these passages helpful or not helpful in thinking about what marriage should be like in the 21st century?

was head of the household. Verse 23 reflects this cultural pattern. Being head of the household meant cherishing and protecting the wife. This role meant loving one's wife as one's own body, the same way that Christ loves the church.

Paul's friendship with Priscilla and Aquila provides another New Testament look at marriage. Throughout Acts 18 Priscilla and Aquila are mentioned together. They left Rome by order of Emperor Claudius and worked together in Corinth as tentmakers. When Priscilla and Aquila heard a Jew named Apollos preach there, together they "explained the Way of God to him more accurately" (18:26). In this biblical model of marriage husband and wife worked side by side.

Divorce. In Hebrew society the man had the right of divorce if his wife no longer pleased him. Deuteronomy 24:1-4 requires him to give her a written bill of divorce to free her to marry someone else. This regulation protected her from being stoned to death for adultery.

The prophet Malachi (Malachi 2:10-16) wrote to the people of Jerusalem after the Exile. Members of prominent families were returning from Babylonia to their homeland without property, money, or position. Many of the men divorced their Jewish wives to marry foreign women of status and money. Malachi spoke out strongly against such faithlessness. The survival of the divorced women and of the traditional faith of the ancestors was at risk.

> Read Deuteronomy 24:1-4; Mark 10:2-12; Matthew 5:31-32; and Malachi 2:13-16. In what ways are these passages helpful or not helpful in thinking about divorce in the 21st century?

Over the centuries, the culture accepted the view that a man could divorce his wife for any reason. Jesus challenged this practice in Mark 10:2-12. The Pharisees wanted to test Jesus to see if he would contradict the law found in Deuteronomy 24:1-4. Jesus responded with Genesis 2:24, in which God blessed the union between male and female. Jesus understood the marriage bond as not to be broken, no matter what human laws and regulations allowed. In Mark 10:11-12, Jesus granted equal power to women. As her husband's property, a woman could only ask her husband for a divorce. Jesus' teaching challenges this understanding by giving the woman power not given in the law of Moses.

Christians value the marriage covenant and expression of love, mutual support, and shared fidelity between a husband and wife. Christians believe that God blesses such unions. Ask yourself the following questions. Write responses in the spaces provided after each question.

What does *love* mean to you?

Faith Matters for Young Adults: Living the Faith

What are some examples of "mutual support"?

What do you think "shared fidelity" means? Is shared fidelity an important issue for you? Why or why not?

Christians also recognize that in some cases marriage partners are estranged beyond reconciliation. Divorce, while regrettable, may be the only alternative. Divorce is painful. Christians are called to compassionate care and ministry to those who have experienced divorce and to the families affected by its broken-ness. Read the following questions and write responses in the spaces provided.

What do you think "estranged beyond reconciliation" means? What might be some causes for such estrangement?

What do you think persons going through a divorce feel?

What are some ways the church can minister to divorced persons? What are some ways the church can minister to the children of divorced persons?

A God of New Beginnings

Christian faith is a resurrection faith. It is all about new life given as a gift in Jesus Christ. Both marriage and divorce provide occasions for people to experience the power of new life. One thing is absolutely certain—in marriage and in divorce, God loves us, supports us, and never abandons us. God is with us when we marry and gives support and blessing to our unions. When the marriage does not work and divorce occurs, God still chooses to be with us. God gives us what we need to move through the pain and toward a new life. Nothing separates us from God's love.

– CLOSING WORSHIP —

Pray together the following prayer:
"Caring and reconciling God, you are a God of new beginnings and rising again. Teach us to believe our covenant relationships can rise again from struggles and misunderstandings to new strength and deeper commitment. Teach us to believe that when our covenants fail, you are with us. You care for us. You hurt with us. Show us new life in our failures, God; in the name of your son Jesus. Amen."

Session 11

How Can I Forgive?

Pamela Dilmore

FOCUS This session will help young adults understand the importance of forgiveness in their relationships with others.

‒ GATHERING ‒

Prepare three graffiti sheets by writing the following open-ended sentences on posterboard or large sheets of white paper. Allow space to write endings to the sentences. On one sheet write "Forgiveness is. . . ." On the second sheet write "Forgiving others is like. . . ." On the third sheet write "When I forgive, I feel. . . ." Place these sheets on a wall. Have crayons or colored markers available. Group members will write or draw responses to each of the open-ended sentences. In the large group, tell one another about what you have written.

Pray together the following prayer:
"Forgiving and loving God, guide us as we explore the challenges of forgiveness. Help us to grow in our understanding and in our capacity to forgive; in Christ we pray. Amen."

Journeys and Luggage

How can I forgive? All humans have experienced pain inflicted by other persons or situations. Our faith teaches the importance of forgiving persons or situations that cause us pain. Christian teachings about forgiveness are challenging. The Gospel of Matthew offers a particularly challenging one. "For if you forgive others their trespasses, your heavenly Father will also forgive you; but if you do not forgive others, neither will your Father forgive your trespasses" (Matthew 6:14-15). God's forgiveness depends on our forgiving others? What does that mean? How can we forgive others when we hurt so badly? Forgiving others sometimes feels like giving up and giving in. Does forgiving others mean I have to allow others to walk all over me as though I were a doormat?

On our life journeys we carry emotional and spiritual luggage that interferes with our ability to experience the healing forgiveness of God. When we can let go of our luggage of anger, hurt, and frustration through the act of forgiveness, our life journey is lighter and freer.

Think about a typical journey in your life. How much luggage do you take? How much do you need? What could you leave behind to make your journey easier? Imagine a journey with lots of luggage, with little luggage, and with no luggage. Write responses to the statements that follow.

Picking up my luggage feels like . . .

Ahead of time gather together several pieces of luggage. Put something in the luggage to make it heavy. Create a pathway in your learning area. If you have a small amount of space, find a place inside or outside the church to create a pathway. Use chairs or furniture to create obstacles on the path so that the luggage will bump. Be creative with your pathway. Make the end of the path near the beginning of the path. Tell group members they must remain on the path.

Group members, one at a time, pick up all the luggage and carry it as you "journey" on the pathway. When you get to the end, put the luggage down and make the same journey without carrying it. Discuss responses to the statements in the main text.

Putting down all my luggage feels like . . .

Faith Matters for Young Adults: Living the Faith

On my life journey, my luggage is like . . .

In order to lighten my luggage, I need to forgive . . .

What Happens When We Forgive?

Find a partner. Talk together about what you have written or drawn regarding your early perceptions, understandings, ideas, or beliefs about Christian faith. Did these change as you became an adult? If so, how? To what do you attribute the changes?

The sense of the word *forgive* used in the New Testament is to let go or send away. The word in Greek expresses "an energy of sending forcefully away." The amazing thing about this understanding of forgiveness is that it has little to do with the one who is forgiven. The act of forgiving energizes our own spiritual and emotional health. It is not intended to control the feelings and actions of other people. Forgiving others certainly will change the way we relate to them, but forgiving may or may not affect their actions.

When we forgive, we let go, separate ourselves from, and send away the negative energies of the pain, bitterness, frustration, and anger we feel toward persons. We separate persons from their actions. We can will good for persons while we at the same time disapprove of their actions.

Can I Forgive This?

Knowing how the process of forgiveness operates does not mean that forgiving is easy. Consider the persons and actions in the following list. Write "yes," "no," or "maybe" to indicate how you might respond to forgiving each person.

– a child who kills a parent
– a parent who neglects a child

- a parent who batters a child
- someone who steals your credit cards
- someone who steals all your money
- someone whom you trust lies to you
- someone who spreads gossip about you
- someone who accuses you falsely
- someone who makes fun of you
- someone who wrecks your car
- someone who is uncooperative
- someone who is insensitive to your feelings
- the murder of six million Jews in World War II

What Does the Bible Say?

The teachings of Jesus offer a sense of spiritual freedom in the act of forgiveness. Forgiveness is a matter of the heart and offers release from fear and bitterness.

Matthew 6:14-15. Jesus' teaching in this passage tells us that God forgives those who forgive others. Forgiving others removes the barriers that prevent us from experiencing the forgiveness of God. Jesus understands the way the human heart sets up barriers with strong negative feelings directed toward others. With such feelings clogging the spirit, how can an awareness of God's "release," that is, "letting go" of our shortcomings or hurts toward others or toward God, get through? Could Jesus be saying we prevent ourselves from experiencing the freedom of knowing that we are forgiven?

> Find a partner. Read Matthew 6:14-15. What challenges you about this Scripture? What insights does it offer to you about forgiveness?

Matthew 18:21-22. When Peter asked how many times to forgive, Jesus challenged traditional views by focusing on the limitless grace and mercy of God. Those who would live a Kingdom life should show limitless grace and mercy to others. Peter was generous in his suggestion of seven times, but Jesus said to be limitless. Do we want to experience the freedom of forgiving only seven times? Jesus' expansion of this number was figurative. By expanding the actual number, Jesus stretches the mind to help us understand that acts of forgiveness are beyond numbering. Forgiveness is a matter of the heart.

> Find a partner. Read Matthew 18:21-22. What challenges you about this Scripture? What insights does it offer to you about forgiveness?

Luke 17:3-4. Forgiveness does not mean accepting another's injustice or wrongdoing. Forgiveness does not mean giving others license to act in hurtful or destructive ways. Wrong actions should be named, and we should speak out against them. Jesus says "rebuke" persons who do wrong. Tell them the action is wrong. If they repent or turn again to right action and the ways of God, forgive or let go of the offense. Again, as in Matthew 18:21-22, forgiveness is not limited; it is boundless. Grace is unlimited.

> Find a partner. Read Luke 17:3-4. How do you think God feels about someone who does something to cause pain or hurt to someone else? In what ways is it helpful or not helpful to separate persons from actions when we are challenged to forgive? In what ways, if any, does Luke 17:3-4 help you in your need to forgive others?

Romans 12:14-21. This passage gives Paul's understanding of the marks of a true Christian. It deals with the ideas of "enemy" and "vengeance" and implicitly "forgiveness" in terms of actions, both what Christians should and should not do. Forgiveness is more than a feeling; it generates choices and action. It cleans the spirit for positive, Christian action. Letting go does not mean justice should not or will not be done. Letting go means giving the con-

> Read aloud Romans 12:14-21. Form two teams. Team 1 list all the "do" instructions in Romans 12:14-21. Team 2 list all the "do not" instructions in Romans 12:14-21. Report your lists to the entire group. Discuss: What does the word *bless* mean to you? the word *curse*? What is the most difficult of Paul's teachings for you to practice on the "do" list? the least difficult? What is the most difficult of Paul's teachings on the "do not" list? the least difficult? In your life what does it mean to overcome evil with good?

Session 11: How Can I Forgive?

trol to God. Romans 12:19 implies forgiveness in the instruction to "leave room" for God to act. Let go of vengeful feelings and actions. Send them away from you. Allow space for God's good to overcome evil.

An Imaginary Journey

Imagine that you are going to visit someone who is wise and who has your respect. You need to ask for their advice or wisdom. Who is this person in your life? Where are you when you are with them? What does the place where you are look like? smell like? sound like? What are you doing? How do you feel while you are with this person? Imagine yourself asking the following questions and listening to the responses of this person. Write what you imagine the responses to be:

Why should I forgive? Your wise person says,

What happens if I cannot forgive and forget? Your wise person says,

Does God expect me always to forgive? Your wise person says,

Should I forgive others only when they ask me to? Your wise person says,

Can I love others if I cannot forgive? Your wise person says,

Thank your wise person. Return home. Describe what you need to do at home.

An Ongoing Process

Forgiveness is an ongoing process of letting go and sending away the painful inner feelings one harbors. Allowing such feelings to sit like large ships in the harbor of our heart clogs up that harbor and harms our emotional, physical, and spiritual health. We do not deny such feelings; we identify with them and send them sailing into God's care.

— CLOSING WORSHIP —

Pray together the following prayer:
"Loving and forgiving God, we thank you for the gift of Jesus the Christ who shows us what forgiveness can mean in our lives. Teach us to believe that as we forgive, we are healed; in the name of Jesus we pray. Amen."

Session 12

How Can I Accept Forgiveness?

Pamela Dilmore

FOCUS This session will help young adults understand how to accept forgiveness from others and from God.

— GATHERING —

Greet one another as you arrive, then write an ending to the following open-ended sentence: "Accepting forgiveness means_____." Tell one another about your sentence endings.

Pray together the following prayer.
"Forgiving God, be with us as we look at our own need to be forgiven; in the forgiving love of Christ, we pray. Amen."

Accepting Forgiveness

Do I need to accept forgiveness? Why? How? From whom? What difference will being forgiven make in my life? Accepting forgiveness from God and others energizes our lives. It clears our pathways so that we may walk. Accepting God's forgiveness means accepting and participating in the energy of God's healing love.

Sometimes it is more difficult to accept forgiveness from others and from God than it is to forgive. In the deep places of our spirits, we often have more compassion for others than for ourselves. At other times we accuse or blame others for wrongdoing in order to avoid dealing with our own need for forgiveness. God offers healing and wholeness at these times and in these deep places when we accept God's love, forgiveness, and salvation offered through Jesus the Christ.

What is it like to accept forgiveness? Below is a list of analogies. Read them and check the ones that best describe for you what it is like to accept forgiveness.

___ flying with eagles
___ floating in a perfectly calm ocean
___ driving on a straight, smooth road
___ sitting on a mountaintop
___ sitting in a rocking chair on a front porch
___ walking in a colorful garden
___ going fishing on a workday
___ looking at a list of tasks and finding everything checked off
___ taking off a backpack
___ putting down an armload of books
___ other?

Christian Words Related to Forgiveness

Christianity uses words such as *sin, confession, repentance, forgiveness,* and *grace* to describe the mystery of healing and growth God gives in Christ. What do these words mean? What is *forgiveness of sin*? Do we have to confess our sin in order to be forgiven? How do we know when we have been forgiven, and how do we respond?

In a broad sense sin is the condition of feeling separated or alienated from God. Specific actions that cause this condition

Cover a cube-shaped cardboard box with white paper. The box should be large but manageable enough to toss as though it were a large die. Write each of the following questions on a surface of the box so that each surface has a question: "What is sin?" "What is confession?" "What is repentance?" "What is forgiveness?" "What is grace?" "What is a response to forgiveness?"

Group members sit in a circle. Toss the cube from one member to another. Answer the question that is on top of the cube. Discuss responses.

are often called *sins*. *Confession* is acknowledging our alienation from God and the actions or situations that create this condition. It is diving into the wrecked places of our spirits and offering the things we discover there to the care of God, so that they no longer have power over us. *Forgiveness* may be thought of as the activity or energy of God through Christ that restores us, heals us, reconciles us, gives us awareness of and the ability to participate in God's love. Another word for this is *grace*.

"I Don't Remember"

The following story illustrates the grace of God that we can experience when we accept forgiveness.

A pastor of a church committed a great sin. For years he grieved over the sin. Remembering his sin caused him great emotional and spiritual anguish.

In the congregation was a woman who spent much time in prayer. She often told the pastor what God had said to her during her time of prayer. One day, in exasperation, the pastor said, "The next time you talk with God, ask him to tell you about my great sin!"

> What does the story say about the relationship between forgiving and forgetting? In what ways do you identify with the way the pastor did not accept forgiveness but held on to the memory of his sin? What does the story say to you about God's nature? about human nature?

The next Sunday the woman went up to the pastor after the worship service and said, "I talked to God this week, and I asked him to tell me about your great sin, Reverend."

The pastor asked hesitatingly and a little mockingly, "Well? What did God say?"
"God said, 'I don't remember.'"

(*From Illustrations Unlimited,* by James H. Hewett; Tyndale House, 1988; page 216)

What Does the Bible Say?

In each of the following Scriptures, specific instructions are given to the people who experience forgiveness. Read the Scriptures and the commentary about each of them. Write responses to the questions in the spaces provided.

John 8:2-11. In this story of a woman caught in adultery, Jesus dealt brilliantly with the scribes and Pharisees and the woman. The scribes and Pharisees wanted to trap Jesus into violating the law so they could condemn him. They dragged a woman caught in adultery before him and reminded him that the law of Moses said she should be stoned to death. Jesus was too shrewd to fall into their trap of disagreeing with the law. Instead, he drove the awareness of the scribes and Pharisees into the stony places of their own spirits. "Let anyone among you who is without sin be the first to throw a stone at her" (8:7). He gave the power to decide back to them. One by one they walked away. Awareness of one's own sin is the beginning of healing. Jesus offered the scribes and Pharisees a gift.

Jesus then stood and asked the woman a question that forced her to look at the reality of the situation. "Where are they? Has no one condemned you? . . . Neither do I" (8:10-11). Awareness of the freedom of being forgiven enables one to walk into a new way of life. "Go your way, and . . . do not sin again" (8:11). Accept forgiveness and make new choices.

What instructions were given to the woman caught in adultery? What, if anything, do these instructions say to you about needed changes in your behavior or life?

Mark 2:1-12. Healing the paralyzed man provides the occasion to focus on God's power and grace and what might happen as we choose to participate in God's power and grace, especially when it means helping others. The story also reveals the connection between spiritual and physical healing.

The friends of the paralyzed man chose to bring him to Jesus and boldly lower him through the roof. The paralyzed man depended on his friends, and he chose to accept their efforts on behalf of his healing. Jesus commented on the faith of the friends and forgave the man's sin, offending the scribes in the crowd. They believed only God could forgive sins. The issue is God's power.

Jesus responded, "Which is easier, to say . . . , 'Your sins are forgiven,' or to say, 'Stand up and take your mat and walk'?" (2:9). The answer is that saying one's sins are forgiven is easier to say, since no physical evidence is necessary to demonstrate the result. Saying, "Walk," requires the paralyzed man to accept God's power to forgive and heal and to choose to walk. All will see the result.

The connections between spiritual and physical healing have been observed for thousands of years. Scribe, friend, or paralytic, we choose whether or not we will accept and participate in God's forgiving, healing power.

What instructions were given to the paralyzed man? What, if anything, do these instructions say to you about needed changes in your behavior or life?

Luke 7:36-50. The woman who anointed Jesus' feet with her tears and dried them with her hair demonstrated with her actions the forgiveness she had experienced. She accepted forgiveness. She felt its meaning and power. She responded in gratitude with loving action. Simon the Pharisee was concerned because the woman was a sinner and her touch made Jesus "unclean." Jesus

Faith Matters for Young Adults: Living the Faith

then told a story that named the deep connection between love and forgiveness. One who is forgiven much, loves much. Again Jesus attended to the need of the one in front of him. He named reality for the woman and for all humans. "Your sins are forgiven. . . . Your faith has saved you; go in peace" (7:48, 50). Continue life in wholeness, health, and serenity.

Form three teams. Team 1 read John 8:2-11; Team 2 read Mark 2:1-12; and Team 3 read Luke 7:36-50. What does your team's Scripture teach about forgiveness, accepting forgiveness, and life choices? Rewrite the story in your team's Scripture as though it were happening today. Present your modern stories to the entire group.

What instructions were given to the woman who washed Jesus' feet? What, if anything, do these instructions say to you about needed changes in your behavior or life?

Recall an experience of accepting forgiveness from another person or God. Remember what you felt and thought. Write briefly about that experience in the space provided.

For what do you need to accept forgiveness today?

How might you respond to forgiveness from others? from God? What difference would it make in your day-to-day life?

Session 12: How Can I Accept Forgiveness?

God's Gift

God's forgiveness does not depend on what we do or whether we feel something. Instead, it is a gift revealed and offered to us through Christ. Knowledge of being forgiven comes as we accept the gift and live it day by day.

– CLOSING WORSHIP –

Read aloud Psalm 32:1-7. Pray the following prayer:
"God of hope and new life, we thank you for the gift of forgiveness and healing you give through the Christ. We accept it, and we praise you. We ask for your guidance as we try to live in and share the energy of your love; in the name of Jesus. Amen."

S e s s i o n   1 3

How Can God Mend a Broken Heart?

Larry F. Beman

FOCUS This session will help young adults discover ways God responds to the trauma in their life resulting from broken relationships.

– GATHERING —

Ahead of time create a "broken heart" using a large sheet of red poster paper. Group members will write thoughts or feelings that the image of the broken heart suggests to them on this poster paper.

Pray together the following prayer:
"Caring God, be with us as we recall times when our hearts have been broken. Help us to discover your healing presence when we have been hurt; in Christ we pray. Amen."

What Is Going On Inside This Broken Heart?

Look at this picture of a broken heart. Write answers to the question, What is going on inside this broken heart?

Think about these questions: Have you ever had a broken heart? Have you experienced the loss of a significant relationship? A large percentage of marriages dissolve in divorce, many within the first five years. Persons experience the loss of important friends. Parents die unexpectedly. Accidents and suicide damage the human soul. Have you experienced any of these? If so, try to remember what helped you in your grieving and in your healing. Write responses in the spaces provided after the questions:

What did others do that helped you?

What hurt you or made you angry?

Where did you find hope? disillusionment? acceptance? alienation?

How was your faith important to you? Where did you find God in the midst of your pain?

The issues suggested by these questions are the issues that this session touches. Broken hearts are common. So, how do we "get over it"? How do we find pathways to healing and wholeness? Our era is not the only one in which relationships have been strained and broken. The Old and New Testaments both record their share of tragedies. However, along with the pain they offer a message of hope.

As I look back on my own recovery from a time of a broken heart, I am aware that the healing process worked for me much as it does for anyone else. Time, patience, awareness of emotions, and close friends all were important for me. Yet I also discovered that I lived with an extra level of "being." Somewhere in the middle of it all, I felt the incredible presence of God's grace filling me, bandaging me, empowering me, and nudging me onward. God's being in my life made an enormous difference, and I believe I am a changed person as a result.

Broken Heart Feelings

Experiencing a broken heart generates a wide range of emotions. Which of the broken heart feelings in the list come closest to describing your experience? Add to these statements in a way that makes them your own. For example, "I feel cheated! I feel as if an important part of my life was taken away, and it's not fair!"

> Find a partner. Talk about your broken heart feelings. When have you had this feeling? What did you do to overcome it?

"There is a huge empty hole in my soul."

"I have been cheated."

"I am frightened. What will happen to me now?"

"I feel guilty. If only. . . ."

"I'm so angry! Why did she do that to me?"

"I have been rejected."

"It's all his fault!"

How Do We Respond to People Who Have a Broken Heart?

We all know more than one person who has experienced a broken heart. It takes time and energy to listen to or be present to someone who is hurting. Sometimes our responses to them are helpful, and other times they are not. Perhaps we have heard people say something like, "I don't know what I would have done if my friends had not been around," or "No one talked to me after the breakup." Well-meaning friends may say things like, "You are better off without her," or "What did you do to run him off?" In the space provided, make a list of ways people respond to those who are hurting:

Share with the entire group your list of ways people respond to those with a broken heart. Create a master list in the group. Which ones are helpful? Which ones are hurtful? Why? What do you think are appropriate ways to respond to persons who are brokenhearted?

What Does the Bible Say?

Read each of the Scriptures in the following list. What do they say to you about healing a broken heart? Make notes in the spaces provided after each Scripture.

"Cast your burden on the LORD,
    and he will sustain you" (Psalm 55:22).
Read Psalm 55:1-5, 22.

"He heals the brokenhearted,
   and binds up their wounds" (Psalm 147:3).
Read Psalm 147:1-6.

"Jesus began to weep" (John 11:35).
Read John 11:28-36.

"To the thirsty I will give water as a gift from the spring of the water of life" (Revelation 21:6b).
Read Revelation 21:1-7.

Psalms 34; 55; 147. The dominant theme of Scripture is that God lives among those who are hurting, binding their wounds and healing them. The psalms of the Old Testament were the hymns of God's people called Hebrews. Like many hymns, these songs were born out of struggle and heartache. Time after time, the songwriters told stories of agony and trauma. Time after time, they concluded with a cry of faith. The writer of Psalm 34 said,
   "I sought the LORD, and he answered me,
      and delivered me from all my fears . . .
   The LORD is near to the brokenhearted,
      and saves the crushed in spirit" (Psalm 34:4, 18).

Then, in Psalm 147, the psalmist sings,
"How good it is to sing praises to our God; . . .
He heals the brokenhearted,
and binds up their wounds" (Psalm 147:1b, 3).

Have an assortment of supplies available (for example, modeling clay, construction paper, paper clips, paper cups, scissors, colored markers or crayons). Form four teams. Each team select one of the Scriptures. Read the Scripture. What does this Scripture passage say about grief? According to this Scripture, how does God respond to the brokenhearted? If you were a person with a broken heart, how would you react to this passage? Use the materials to create a symbol to illustrate the theme of this passage. When everyone has finished, ask for a representative from each team to report to the group by summarizing the message of that team's Scripture passage and describing its symbol.

John 11:28-44; Revelation 21:1-7. This theme of wholeness in the midst of trauma carries into the New Testament. At Lazarus's grave Jesus wept and then brought new life out of decay (John 11:35, 43-44). The Book of Revelation was written as a message of hope to those who were being arrested, persecuted, and executed because of their faith. In the midst of this unspeakable horror, the writer spoke for God, saying, "I am making all things new. . . . To the thirsty I will give water as a gift from the spring of the water of life" (Revelation 21:5-6).

Ingredients for Healing

People are not helpless when it comes to practices that will help the healing process. Some "ingredients for healing" follow. Review the list. Place an exclamation mark (!) by those ingredients you believe are important. Place an X by those ingredients you believe are faulty or irrelevant. Place a question mark (?) by those ingredients about which you are undecided or have questions.

Faith Matters for Young Adults: Living the Faith

___ Be patient with yourself. Healing takes a great deal of time. Do not make any major decisions for at least a year and a half.

___ Find friends you can trust. Lean on them for support. They will be there for you just as you are there for them.

___ If you are depressed, ask, What is making me angry? Find ways to use depression as an opportunity for growth.

___ Have a "pity party," real or imagined. Drape the room in black. It's OK to feel bad. Make the best of it.

> How did you respond to each of the "ingredients for healing"? Which ones seem most helpful? least helpful? Why?

___ Cry. Tears are agents of healing and release. Jesus wept; so can you. Give yourself permission to cry.

___ Look for signs of God's presence with you. God did not cause this tragedy; but God and you can work together to discover a rich, new life.

___ Remember that wounds will scar, but the scar tissue is often stronger than the original skin.

___ Reach out to help someone else. It will give you a chance to let go of your own hurts for a while.

___ Ask for the help of a trained counselor. They are often God's ambassadors of healing.

___ Lean into your pain. Don't try to avoid it. The paradox is that your pain will go away more quickly if you live in it rather than if you run away from it.

___ Be good to yourself. Treat yourself. Get lots of rest. Exercise regularly. Do something for fun. Avoid excesses of alcohol, drugs (prescription or otherwise), work, or other forms of avoidance.

___ Remember that the holidays will be different. They can be a time of crisis, or you can use them as an opportunity for small but significant change.

___ Pray. In your own way and style, focus on the One who is the center of all life.

God Is Near

After our conversations in this session, how would you now answer the question, How can God mend a broken heart? Write a response in the space provided:

Healing happens in many ways for those who have a broken heart. However, one thing is certain. As people heal, God is present. We are never alone. God gives us the strength we need to get through whatever we must as we recover from a broken heart.

– CLOSING WORSHIP –

Pray silently for a few moments. If you feel moved to do so, speak aloud the first name of someone you know who is grieving. Respond together to each name by saying, "God, heal the brokenhearted and bandage their wounds." Close the prayer time by praying together the Lord's Prayer.